FOR THE CHILDREN OF ABRAHAM: Scripture's Wisdom

By the Same Author

Shabbat

FOR THE CHILDREN OF ABRAHAM: Scripture's Wisdom

Charles Vernoff

• • •

Ellipsis Imprints
2021

. . .
Ellipsis Imprints
Durham, England
. . .

Twitter: @EllipsisImprint

For the Children of Abraham: Scripture's Wisdom
Print edition ISBN: 978-1-8380723-3-9
Ebook edition ISBN: 978-0-4635980-3-0

Cover photo by Marleen de Kramer.
Cover design by Sara L. Uckelman.

First printing 2021

Contents

For You, the Reader: A Prologue

FIVE distinct but overlapping readerships may well find this book of significant, perhaps life changing, value: spiritual seekers; Jews and Christians; participants in the Abrahamic trialogue; college students for which this is an assigned course text; and academicians of various sorts. Feel free to read whichever section or sections of the Prologue may apply to you, or none at all. You may also wish to peruse the Prologue after reading the main text. A justification for reading the Prologue regardless is that it offers a helpful introductory orientation to the task ahead. In any case, the author's devout hope is that these chapters will make their way to all of these intended audiences and fructify among them:

Spiritual Seekers

This book aims to reach the heart and soul of every genuine seeker after spiritual truth, whether individuals or those studying in groups. Widespread seeking for such truth is a well-established phenomenon of our times. During the 1960s, a spiritual hunger exploded within the youth generation that in one form or another has persisted ever since. That hunger was initially tied to crises of confidence in America due to the assassination of President Kennedy together with the Viet Nam War. Not surprisingly, young Americans turned elsewhere for hope and inspiration—principally to Eastern traditions. By the 1970s, the quest for a more perfect world had given rise to a body of "New Agers" open to everything from Eastern religion to wisdom from alien extraterrestrials to various forms of magic and divination. More recently, New Age spiritual seekers have once again admitted the Western spiritual tradition into their purview, prodded by interests in the "secret history" of Jesus ostensibly conveyed in *The Da Vinci Code* and other books, the Sufi poetry of Rumi, Kabbalah, Gnosticism, computer-analyzed Bible codes, and so forth.

To the individual seeker, whether inclined toward a New Age disposition or not, this book will offer a startling proposal. Right under the gaze of Western Civilization, so to speak, has lain for over two thousand years a religious corpus that bears its own astonishing warrant of origin from the traditional, supernatural personal God of Abrahamic religion. Familiar writings, hitherto supposed universally to constitute a miscellaneous collection, disclose an extraordinary pattern of meaningful organization that can plausibly be ascribed neither to chance nor to human devise. At one stroke, this collection of texts becomes a profoundly useful integrated spiritual handbook and a witness to the reality of its Divine source. These texts comprise the third section of the Hebrew Scriptures, the Writings—*Ketuvim* in Hebrew, the *Hagiographa* in Greek.

The notion presented here requires no prior faith commitment and pleads no special case. It appeals to nothing more mystical than an ordinary sense of the statistical likelihood of highly improbable occurrences. For example, sand grains thrown from a bucket into the air over a beach boardwalk would surely not land on the ground in the form of an exquisite landscape. On the other hand, it is up to each reader to judge the merits of the claim and—only if found worthy—to become convinced.

Jews and Christians

Spiritual seekers spawned by '60s also included the hippie "Jesus people," a major stimulus to the new Evangelical Christianity that now claims some 60,000,000 adherents in America alone. One striking mark of this transformed Evangelical spirit is its total reversal in attitude toward the Jewish People and the

State of Israel, of which Evangelicals are now the most ardent friends in the world. But, Evangelical Christian or otherwise, if this book addresses every sincere individual spiritual seeker, it has a special claim on the attention of believers already committed to the God of Abraham, whether they be Jewish, Christian or Muslim. For believing Jews and Christians in particular, the Ketuvim are unquestionably Holy Writ. This book will address these groups' need for *spiritual nourishment*, whether read individually, in an independent fellowship or in a synagogue or church study group. For group study, see the suggestions below addressed to an Abrahamic trialogue study group, but equally applicable to a single faith venture. It is safe to say that the approach to the texts herein is likely to prove original, illuminating and personally helpful to many adherents of the Judaic and Christian traditions, presenting familiar texts from an utterly unfamiliar angle of vision that may disclose much missed by other perspectives—possibly even revealing the Ketuvim in an entirely new light. Thus this material may be approached by believing Jews and Christians as *lectio divina*—the Catholic term for inspirational spiritual reading. The following section should be read closely by those embarking on single faith group work as well as those in interfaith discussions.

The Abrahamic Trialogue

Over the last several decades, accelerated by the disaster of 9/11, a vital and novel conversation has been initiated among some Muslims, Christians and Jews about religious commonalities and differences. More recently, any number of scattered groups engaged in this trialogue among Abrahamic traditions have adopted the name "Children of Abraham," a felicitous term that has also appeared in print. It seems that as the political landscape becomes more menacing, with heightened armed conflict among too many adherents to these traditions, those who seek the path of mutual understanding rather than mutual annihilation have intensified their efforts toward productive interchange.

The sincerity of this effort notwithstanding, it is no easy matter to move beyond the stage of superficially presenting one's convictions toward the building of real bonds of Abrahamic fellowship, based on values deeply held by the traditions themselves. Declaring and discussing beliefs is a somewhat precarious venture, given different degrees of expertise among participants and the danger of reaching a dead end once such "sharing" is complete. A further, more searching and meaningful phase of trialogical exchange could be facilitated by nothing so much, perhaps, as a *text* of universal Abrahamic monotheism to be studied jointly and critically. Intense and probing reflection upon such a text could concretize both similarities and differences among the traditions, opening the door to vastly more profound mutual understanding, more informed questioning, realistic bridge building, cooperation, a sense of common purpose and genuine fellow feeling. But where might such a text be found?

All three traditions acknowledge the Hebrew Scriptures, known to Jews as *TaNaKH*, to be the initial written historical revelation of Abrahamic monotheism. TaNaKH is an acronym for *Torah* (Instruction), *Nevi'im* (Prophets) and *Ketuvim* (Writings). The third section of Tanakh, the Ketuvim, contains five books technically classified by scholars as Wisdom Literature. Wisdom Literature, concerned with imparting an understanding of how to lead a successful life, is a genre widespread throughout the entire ancient Near East. Both Babylonia and Egypt, among other cultures, developed such literature. The ubiquity and generic similarity of Wisdom Literature throughout this ancient region already bears a hint of universality.

Even more promising, a careful interpretive reading of the Ketuvim reveals that an additional four texts have a universal purport, despite inevitably featuring Jewish characters, that can be gleaned by all believers in One transcendent Creator. Thus fully nine books in this collection appear to display the "wisdom" character of universal spiritual counsel, in this case especially to Abrahamic monotheists. The remaining four books of the Ketuvim—Ezra, Nehemiah, and Chronicles I/II—consist of a more parochial subject matter: the contiguous history of the Israelite/Jewish People before and after the Babylonian Exile. The role of these texts in the Ketuvim raises a different sort of question that we will address in its proper place.

Given that nine Ketuvim texts possess a degree of sanctity and relevance for all three Abrahamic traditions, with Islam regarding David, putative author of Psalms, as a major prophet, as is his son Solomon—Suleiman in Arabic—and venerating the Iranian tomb of Esther, the Ketuvim would seem to offer precisely that literature whose vigorous and dynamic study by the "Children of Abraham" could galvanize a deeper new phase beyond the simple sharing of beliefs. In the Ketuvim, Abrahamic monotheists might find a solid textual foundation for an evident yet still elusive fellowship. This book will argue that the nine Ketuvim texts may, in fact, constitute a unifying, universal spiritual guide for actual living that might be conscientiously explored, embraced and affirmed by all Abrahamic believers in One Creator. And, indeed, its amazing organization seems clearly to show the mark of the Creator's Providential hand. To unlock the secrets of the Ketuvim as divinely revealed Abrahamic guidebook, and thereby lay the foundation for a genuine Fellowship of Abraham, this volume will aspire to serve as key.

At the same time, the force of the analysis that follows depends in part upon the fact that no effort has been made toward achieving some sort of Abrahamic "homogenization" that purees Hebrew texts into an imagined trialogic common denominator. The interpretation is by a believing (howbeit universally minded) Jew, rendering texts that are most specifically part of the heritage of Israel, even though the current presentation aims at a larger audience. For that reason, there are occasional remarks on the Judaic context of the Ketuvim—but also comments, when appropriate, providing comparison with other, including non-Abrahamic, religions. It is precisely in and through their very Israelitic particularity, by which alone these texts speak to members of other Abrahamic traditions, that we can recognize the signature of One God Who is increasingly acknowledged as the common source of three different yet sibling—and perhaps complementary, even *interdependent*—religious traditions.

It must be noted that there are other "children of Abraham" than those adhering to the three major traditions. These include B'nei Noach (usually former Christians who undertake to live by the seven Noachide laws of the Torah, as defined in the Oral Torah handed down by the Rabbis), Bahá'í and Druze (offshoots of Islam), Karaites and Samaritans (offshoots of the Israelite tradition). There are also, of course, numerous non-orthodox Christian groups. This guidebook is also addressed to all of these who search for Abrahamic community as well as to Jews, Christians and Muslims, and all merit a warm welcome by mainstream Children of Abraham as all together seek pan-Abrahamic truths and fellowship.

College Students

If you are assigned this as a course text, your instructor will of course determine the assigned readings. But you may find it to your advantage, both scholastically and personally, to realize that this material is not just the product of dispassionate scholarship but of the author's very personal, spiritual encounters with the texts discussed. You may wish to open yourself at a deeper level to the message of these chapters and be prepared for the possibility that—academics aside—they might hold something of profound personal and spiritual significance for you as well. The author, in any case, intends to address you personally, soul to soul—with any academic motive far in the background as far as he is concerned. Consider, whether assigned or not, at some point reading this Prologue in its entirety.

Academicians: A Possible Refutation of Deconstruction

Material in this book offers a particular challenge to academics, especially those humanists of every discipline who remain haunted by the lively ghosts of post-modernism and its parasitic offspring, deconstruction. To fathom the depth of this challenge requires briefly weighing in, however belatedly, to the waning debate over the meaning of "post-modern"—a term that originated in a 1967 book about Las Vegas architecture but quickly displayed its resonance with the *Zeitgeist* by spreading elsewhere like wildfire. I suggest that the term, taken seriously, displays an uncanny accuracy. Although the roots of the Modern era can be dated back to the Renaissance or even earlier, the "classic" phase of Modernism was initiated by the French Revolution and ended with World War II: the "post-modern" period, we shall see, begins precisely with that watershed conflict's termination.

The worldview associated with classical Modernism, presiding over the triumph of modern industrial and cybernetic society, was Enlightenment humanism. Humanism is a religion grounded in prematurely messianic faith premises that human nature is already both universally rational and universally good. It denies the reality of evil in favor of mere "maladjustment" and affirms that *reason*, applied to every aspect of life, displays life's "indefinite perfectibility" (an 18th-century term of the French *philosophes*)—i.e., results in inevitable *progress*. The prooftext for humanism's "truth" was rationally engineered *technology* which, despite some negative byproducts, generally appeared to improve human life for well over a century. The credibility of humanism based on the testimony of inevitable progress—together with this religion's denial of evil—collapsed, however, with World War II's *technology of megadeath*, embodied in both Auschwitz and Hiroshima. At this point the humanist faith that modern industrial society had both brilliantly benefited from and supported was fatally undermined, although vestiges live on. The optimistic Modern Era implicitly reached its decisive end with Hiroshima and the world entered the indefinitely extended dreariness of the current *post*-modern epoch.

Strictly speaking, avowed post-modernists are thus post-humanists. But in contemporary global culture, much of the world has embraced aspects of Enlightenment humanism, with modern industrial society as its carrier. Thus the shock waves of the collapse of the Modern Era resonate globally. Although humanism continues to limp along bearing its wounds, few conscientiously affirm its faith premises any longer. Generation X a couple of decades ago announced that there *was* no progressive "future" out there—only a gray nothingness. "Progress" was the last version—albeit a secularized one—of triumphant historical advance toward the future Kingdom of God, posited by *all* Abrahamic traditions: this underscores the vast millennial magnitude of the present *Kulturkrisis*.

With collapse of faith in a positive future for the "modern" world, the past becomes irrelevant since it is of genuine interest only when time is experienced as having coherent direction; with negation of both future and past as significantly addressing humanity, the present becomes an empty vacuum devoid of the contextualizing meaning that only a sense of linear directionality can impart to it. But both past and future have faded away as mere reifications, thereby precluding "meaning." This condition, gradually revealing itself in the wake of World War II, is the general post-modern situation. For those touched by the post-modern ethos, values themselves become emptied of content since their function is to direct decisions toward a future perceived as meaningful. All that now remains of decision is pathetically trivial and arbitrary present time determinations—e.g., the proverbial yuppie trying to "decide" what sort of brie cheese to consume with the evening's wine. Human experience becomes vapid, numbing, disconnected, cynical, narcissistic. Genuine purpose vanishes from life. Motor vehicles as early as the 1970s bore the tellingly despondent, anomic yuppie bumper sticker, "He who dies with the most toys wins." Although life, of course, demands necessary choices—careers, etc.—the salt has lost its savor.

The demise of meaning-laden historical consciousness following World War II (or in America, the '60s) was fortuitously hastened and reinforced by a technological byproduct developed during that conflict: *the computer*. Cybernetic technology has now become so pervasive as to refashion human identity itself, increasingly as a function of electronic power perceived as overmastering the fallibility of human intelligence and strength. Thus "computer time" has come to seem more "real" than mere human, i.e., historical, time. The former is the time of the instantaneous electronic synapse, a kind of "eternal moment" in which *only the present instant exists*. The cybernetic revolution has by now thoroughly penetrated Western temporal consciousness, undergirding the sense that both past and future are mere insubstantial human constructs. As computer time supplants living historical time in human consciousness, past and future are likely to continue their evanescence into flimsy diaphanous abstractions, further dissipating the very possibility of "meaning." The sense of temporal as well as spatial horizon has already all but disappeared since, with the click of a computer key, one can virtually be anywhere in time and space.

As it manifests within the intellectual community, the post-modern ethos is innately *suspicious* of any claims to "meaning," since a sense of meaning can crystallize only with reference to the larger historical unfolding of reality. Such a sense arises from comparing the texture of reality at different historical moments and discovering common themes that operate across extended domains of historical time, e.g., the "meaning" of modernity. Meaning can be explored only through large hypotheses that proffer claims regarding the character of phenomena evident throughout stretches of time. But with collapse of a sense of the reality of past and future themselves, broadscale comparisons that engender such exploratory hypotheses are suspect—and indeed scorned.

What remains are only the disconnected data of the present moment, even if the "present moment" be projected into the historical past. Only investigating such discrete and banal minutiae constitutes legitimate "research" for the post-modern scholar. Large hypotheses can therefore only be the speculative opinions of individuals pursuing a private agenda, i.e., the embodiments of personal "political" positions. One of the few legitimate forms of non-"factual" intellectual exercise for the post-modern mind is therefore "deconstructing" large-scale hypotheses and conceptual systems to uncover the core "political" agendas of their authors. Needless to say, given these convictions, any conversational exchange between purveyors of large idea schemes becomes a futile, absurd and disreputable exercise. Theoretical ideas can no longer be taken seriously.

In the fertile soil of the post-modern situation, deconstruction—its origins ascribed to Derrida and others—could take firm root. Deconstruction, a child of the post-modern ethos, thus scoffs at meaningful discourse, dismissing it as nothing but interaction between the trivially subjective "political" stances of various thinkers, wrapped in layers of obfuscating rhetoric. Nothing therefore remains for humanists to do but to expose such stances and collect minutiae without ascribing particular meaning to them. Thus the preoccupation with "area studies," statistics, etc.—inarguable but effete collections of "pure fact." The only actual ideology capable of surviving the post-modern chill is multiculturalism and its blanket affirmation of the rights of all groups—at least in principle. Thus gender studies, racial studies and the like remain academically acceptable. But larger structures of thought, venturesome hypotheses, succumb helplessly to the post-modern atmosphere of depreciation of human historical consciousness. Consequently, genuine discourse imbued with the intellectual ferment that used to attend it has withered throughout much of the humanities in America and abroad. Needless to say, a minority of scholars and intellectuals continue as before, immunizing themselves to the post-modern ravaging of worthwhile thought. But these holdouts are insufficient to rejuvenate intellectual activity in our time.

Nonetheless post-modernism and its deconstructionist offspring are in fact tragic byproducts of a tragic and epochal civilizational collapse, beginning with World War I and consummated by World War II. Unless they are contested, they prefigure the end of the life of the mind as it has always flourished in Western civilization. Fortunately, beginning to meet the challenge requires no more than the elaboration and true grasp of a *history of actual origins*, adumbrated in the preceding paragraphs. Reengendering actual historical consciousness itself, however, might require a presently almost unimaginable group recovenanting with "the future," adhering to nothing less than an original paradigm such as Abraham's entourage agreeing to follow God to a Promised Land, or America's founding Puritans reenacting the Mosaic covenantal model. Notwithstanding all this, the elemental and principled *refutation* of the adequacy of the post-modern/deconstructionist academic fashion must come through the discursive weapons of the unpersuaded intellect. Amongst those, this book aspires to take its place. The implicit claim of the analysis that follows is simply this: There are levels of data that invite and indeed compel consideration as possible "truth" that can only be captured by the wide mesh of large, imaginative conceptualizations, rather than the narrow strainer of post-modernism/deconstructionism's fundamental limitation to "just the facts." For this narrow mesh, broader possible truths slip through, regarded as imaginary chimera—only discrete facts are real. Yet the interpretation elaborated herein purports to disclose a large, yet essentially straightforward, conceptual structure that makes unique sense out of a collection of Hebrew scriptural texts heretofore considered discrete, unrelated and miscellaneous. If this structure withstands reason's inductive test of high plausibility, it stands in defiance to the presuppositions of the prevailing academic ideology. It constitutes a polite invitation to the post-modern/deconstructionist camp to reconsider its views, whatever the consequences. As such, the analysis may be of value to a wide variety of academicians, whether interested or disinterested, including textual and canonical scholars, historians of religion, philosophers and phenomenologists of religion, psychologists and anthropologists of religion, general philosophers, theologians and historians, hermeneuts and exegetes, structuralists and semioticians, linguists and cognitive scientists, literary analysts and educators—to name some of the more obviously germane disciplines.

Group Study Suggestions

The individual seeker for spiritual understanding is, of course, at liberty to study this book in any way that seems appropriate. But how might a study group of Jews or Christians or an aggregate of Jews, Christians and Muslims (as well as others) in conversation—a group seeking some common identity as Children of Abraham—best utilize this volume as a means of finding a profounder level of mutual appreciation and communion? There is, of course, no final answer to this question and each group is free to work as it will. Nonetheless, these preliminary remarks would be remiss if they failed to offer a model that could be adapted or not as each group pleases.

Any study group would be well served by a designated moderator. This person alone might initially read the Introduction below, informally elaborating a couple of essential points to the entire group: the author's assertion that the nine books to be studied constitute a coherent guidebook for relating to the Creator and the Creation, also the essential role that the Ketuvim play in the tripartite structure of the Tanakh. Each group member should then receive a chart (Introduction, section 2) outlining without explanation the proposed configuration of the nine books.

A minimum of two meetings could be devoted to the study of each book. The first meeting might invite each group member to develop his or her particular interpretation of the text, with only incidental regard to the author's chart. Vigorous debate is entirely appropriate. Before the second meeting, the group should read the author's chapter on the text. The meeting itself could then be dedicated to a discussion of the group's provisional judgment of the author's success in clarifying the text, as well as addressing the group's interpretations, and delineating the text's role in the Ketuvim. An optional third meeting would provide an opportunity for free and open discussion to digest, extend and refine the outcome of the first two meetings. For trialogue groups, any nuances of difference in Judaic, Christian and Islamic views could then be fully aired and an effort made to determine if they might be viewed as complementary and, if so, how. Difficulties can be identified and perhaps bridges built. It is the author's personal and professional opinion that the three traditions differ in a way that, in fact, renders them systematically complementary.

A final meeting might seek an overall assessment of the value of the author's hypothesis, preceded by all members reading the Introduction, Epilogue and appendices in their entirety. Trialogue groups, and others if they wish, may optionally begin each meeting with the second appendix containing a Prayer to the God of Abraham—a prayer for guidance toward a true Fellowship of Abraham.

Together with the first and final meetings, this prescribes a minimal 20-week course of study—subject to modification as the group wishes. Out of many trialogue groups, spreading from location to location, immersed in the encounter with these same Ketuvim scriptures, a true textually-grounded universal Fellowship of Abraham could arise, ready for fuller collaboration in thought, prayer and action toward the preexisting joint goal of preparing and inviting the rule of the One God on earth (cf. Appendix One).

A general word of caution to all readers: This work is intended as a brief and accessible guidebook—even workbook—presenting an entirely new approach to the Ketuvim. It is not a conventional introduction nor a detailed literary analysis, much less an exhaustive work of scholarship. To the contrary, each chapter should be read along with the relevant Ketuvim text, although the suggestion that the latter be read first—with the reader developing his or her own initial interpretation—is a useful one for individuals as well as study groups. The keynote of the author's method is, whenever appropriate, to illumine significant principles rather than exhaustively discuss textual examples. Applying these principles in studying the text will engender the most valuable learning experience for the reader. Thus a few textual examples suffice for Psalms, whereas virtually no typical proverb need be cited in the chapter on that book. On the other hand, a challenging work of philosophical theology such as Job demands an extensive analytic treatment, so that interpretive chapter is the longest in this book. In short, the approach demands involvement, active study and participation by the reader, applying the guidance furnished in each chapter—whether lengthy or brief—to the actual text, which will, with the book's aid, increasingly speak for itself and become more and more a part of the student's own consciousness and internalized spiritual "tool kit."

It should be carefully noted that the systematic structure herein that discerns nine texts of the Ketuvim as constituting an integral "spiritual handbook" should be taken as separate from the many other traditional understandings and uses of texts in the collection. For example the Five Megillot are segregated as books read on particular holidays, the three texts of purported Solomonic authorship are taken as a group, a traditional identifying of certain texts as "Wisdom literature" is a staple of secular scholarship, Lamentations is an indispensable adjunct to the prophecy of Jeremiah to whom its authorship is ascribed, etc. The evaluation of the importance of our "spiritual handbook" approach as a way of reading the Ketuvim is a task for others to undertake.

— 1 —

Introduction

1.1 Discovery of the Structure

THE crucial insights for grasping the organizing pattern for the nine non-historical texts of the Ketuvim, texts that might be classified as *literary-theological*, emerged through happenstance. As a young college teacher of comparative religion with emphasis in Judaica, I had to teach two courses in Hebrew Scriptures—which were not my speciality. In approaching the Ketuvim, I fortunately was aware of a famous Talmudic debate over the inclusion of the heavily erotic "Song of Songs" in the scriptural canon. The debate was resolved in favor of inclusion through the argument of Rabbi Akibah, the greatest of his generation, who insisted that *Shir ha-Shirim*, the Song of Songs, was indeed the most sacred book of the entire Scriptures. This was because it presented in allegorical form the ideal, innermost love relationship between God and Israel, represented by Solomon and the Queen of Sheba.

With this initial clue in mind, I turned to my literary training as an undergraduate at the University of Chicago to make further headway. The rubric under which Song of Songs might be placed appeared to be "closeness to God." Proceeding methodically, the next necessary question was whether any other book of the nine fit into this category. A quick inspection led me to the surmise that Psalms, *Tehillim*, indeed belonged under the same rubric. Yet the difference between the two texts was quickly apparent. Whereas Song of Songs presented an image of the *theoretical* ideal of closeness between God and Israel—an eternally binding love—Psalms had a *practical* thrust, providing a large assortment of prayers, meditations and hymns that showed individuals and groups how to reach out toward greater closeness with God from any imaginable concrete human situation. The texts clearly aligned with one another, as does true magnetic north with the compass needle that seeks it.

A next step that appeared obvious enough was to investigate whether any texts of Ketuvim dealt with the situation that contrasts with closeness to God: *distance* from God. A secondary question was whether the theoretical/practical distinction might repeat itself in the category of distance. Not much scrutiny was required to identify Job, *Iyov*, as the text dealing with the theoretical "ideal" of distance from God, with ideal in this case betokening an ultimate theoretical model. In Job, we find *the* most righteous man in the world suffering the torments of *the* most wicked in a situation of uncompromising Divine silence, with God *completely* refusing to explain to Job his situation. Here, surely, was the absolute instance of Divine distance. Could there be a companion practical text? In Lamentations, *Eicha*, complete distance from God—a total breakdown in relationship—results from readily identifiable human transgression; the text specifies the practical path of return to relationship with God from this agonizing extremity of catastrophic collapse. Here, then, was a practical handbook for returning to relationship to God from a situation of vast distance brought on by concrete human sinfulness.

These four texts now assumed the character of a certain schematic geometry: *a vertical axis*. At the top pole was CLOSENESS TO GOD with its theoretical and practical handbooks; at the bottom pole was DISTANCE FROM GOD with its theoretical and practical handbooks. The inescapable question now became: could there be a corresponding *horizontal* axis that might categorize the remaining five books, and if so, what might it be? More than was the case earlier, a leap into the realm of imaginative hypothesis seemed indicated. The first step:

the Abrahamic Deity is most commonly known as the Creator, Whose relationship to Creation is the only way in which He is revealed to humans—we cannot understand God as He understands Himself. Then perhaps the horizontal axis would treat not relationship to the Creator but to the Creation. Together the two intersecting axes might systematically specify all the fundamental relationships that an Abrahamic monotheist might have to these two basic realities, thereby containing the most indispensable spiritual counsel for making one's way wisely and successfully through this mundane world—whose most fundamental existential dimensions are relationship with Creator and Creation.

But what might be the poles of the horizontal axis? These seemed not nearly so obvious as the vertical poles. Here a knowledge of comparative philosophy proves helpful in arriving at a hypothesis. Every major classical philosophical system from Greece to India to China begins with the question of *stability* and *change*, epitomized in the famous pre-Socratic Greek thinker Heraclitus who posed the famous question of whether one could step into the same river twice. The horizontal axis of Creation might address these most basic situations in the realm of typical human worldly experience: then perhaps its poles would be the fundamental categories of "stability and change" or, more precisely, the stable, routine regularities of life in contrast to unpredictable disturbances of that stability by crises involving unexpected change of situation. This hypothesis appeared plausible enough to merit testing.

What texts might occupy the pole of "stability in worldly life?" The practical text seemed unmistakably evident. It is certainly Proverbs, *Mishlei*, which consists largely of useful, pithy nostrums to guide one through the challenges of ordinary, daily experience. But what might be the corresponding theoretical text? Here was the most perplexing interpretive question yet. Nonetheless a clue can be found in the famous Ch. 8 of Proverbs, which is a paean of praise to Wisdom—extolled as God's handmaiden in the Creation and often identified by Jewish sages as

Torah. Wisdom, evidently, is the fountainhead of all the practical nostrums that fill much of the remainder of Proverbs. Clearly, if Wisdom cannot be relied upon as a faithful source of wise counsel, Proverbs contains advice built on sand. Yet there is a book that raises precisely the question of whether Wisdom itself cannot be vanity and folly. That book is Ecclesiastes, *Kohelet*, another text ascribed to Solomonic authorship. Tradition conjectures that Proverbs was written in Solomon's middle years and consists of the advice of a father to a son. Ecclesiastes, on the other hand, embodies the final counsel of Solomon's long and eventful life, written as a man laden with many decades and comprehensively wide-ranging experience.

As we shall see, every ordinary human endeavor as such is pronounced by Solomon to be vanity and futility—*not excluding the quests for wisdom and righteousness themselves*. Even these missions become vanity when pursued out of the ordinary self-centered need to fill one's interior emptiness. So what, then, is the beginning of true wisdom? "*Reishit khokhma yirat Hashem*"—"The beginning of wisdom is awe of the Lord." In other words, any endeavor that emanates from the little self-centered ego is slated for *hevel*, vanity and futility. For the natural ego itself can never be fully gratified. True wisdom, piety and worthy worldly pursuits can be cultivated only when one begins not with oneself but with God—realizing that there is a Creator Who fashioned not only you but a place in the world where alone you can find whatever true contentment and fulfillment is your destiny. Only by your locating that place can genuine happiness be won. Thus Ecclesiastes responds to the "metaquestion" embedded in Proverbs: What if one takes to be "wisdom" itself is an unreliable guide that can lead to futility? The answer is that true Wisdom by definition is always identifiable and reliable because of its grounding in genuine humble awareness of Creator and Creation: true Wisdom begins not with the self but with God. Ecclesiastes thereby assumes the character of "theoretical" text in relation to Proverbs as practical handbook.

Our emerging chart of the literary-philosophical Ketuvim has only one remaining pole—disruptive change that shatters the stable regularities of ordinary life. And only three texts of the literary-philosophical Ketuvim remain. Remarkably enough, each of them is alike a dramatic "tale," a narrative written in literary style strikingly named for an individual protagonist who faces, contends with and ultimately resolves *just such a profound, life-disrupting crisis*: Esther, Ruth, Daniel. Moreover, since we have only the categories of theoretical and practical, two of these books must occupy one niche—itself requiring explanation. We shall determine fairly readily that Ruth and Esther, in their many commonalities and contrasts, together constitute the practical texts and we'll grasp why *two* uniquely are needed. At this point, an astonishing historical note must be cited: Daniel was surely the Ketuvim text which, given its notorious obscurity, I was least familiar with. At the same time only one niche remained in the schema: *the theoretical wisdom pertaining to change*. Since there was no further time to dawdle over the class syllabus, I had no choice but to assign Daniel to that open slot and pray that it would somehow fit when the time came. Let the reader judge the success of this reckless ploy!

As with any classical literature, and certainly with Scripture, the texts reveal more of themselves the more frequently they are visited and the more deeply they are plumbed. In time, the Ketuvim texts will begin to "speak" to one another and yield larger insights. To cite two simple examples: The reader can hardly avoid noticing the persistence of the theme of "remembering and forgetting God," especially prominent in Lamentations, Proverbs and Ecclesiastes. The prevalence of the theme deserves some pondering. A bit more attentiveness is required to notice a fascinating pattern marking the "practical handbooks": with one exception, they are marked by *multiplicity*. This, one may readily infer, is because the practical world presents a vast diversity of concrete situations that call for guidance. Thus there are 150 psalms and many more individual proverbs. An extraordinary example of this appears in the paired books Ruth and Esther that together, as their chapter discusses, define a spectrum that can accommodate an indefinite number of varieties of crisis. The sole exception to this rule is Lamentations, but that is because the task of the text is to delineate the path back to God from a situation of completely shattered relationship. In this case, a "worst case example" among many other possible is appropriate to illustrate the general principle and none could be more fitting than Israel's own most agonizing experience of alienation from the Divine.

One remaining point of some interest involves the order within which the texts at each pole must be considered. From the time the pattern was discovered, I never questioned the fact that the texts dealing with the Creator seemed to require dealing with the theoretical text first whereas, with respect to the texts treating relation to the Creation, it was equally necessary to begin with the practical text. Over a quarter century after this organizing scheme revealed itself, I realized why this was so. The Creator is a transcendent reality and one must first grasp the "ideal dimensions" of understanding God's relationship with humanity before turning to more practical matters. The Creation, on the other hand, is the actual context within which our experience takes concrete shape and is lived out. From this practical experience arises the ultimate theoretical insights that support the very possibility of practical functioning within a world fashioned and indwelled by a transcendent Creator. Thus the contrasting analytic orders.

1.2 The Schematic Organization of the Ketuvim

The preceding section summarizes the thought process that generated a hypothetical schema, assigning niches to each literary-theological text of the Ketuvim. That schema can now be reviewed in its totality of paired *theoretical* and *practical* handbooks (Fig. 1.1).

As we proceed to reflect upon each text of the Ketuvim, it may be helpful to consult this chart in order to determine the place of each text in relation to others. For those with an especially

CLOSENESS TO
THE CREATOR
T: Song of Songs
P: Psalms

STABILITY IN THE CREATION T: Ecclesiastes P: Proverbs	+	CHANGE IN THE CREATION T: Daniel P: Ruth/Esther

DISTANCE FROM
THE CREATOR
T: Job
P: Lamentations

Figure 1.1: The schema

finetuned sensitivity to comparative religious symbolism, it may be worth observing that the structure that clarifies these Judaic texts is *cruciform*, with four poles; and that each pole has two niches for a total of *eight*—a number frequently encountered in Islamic iconography and thought. This may be a trivial curiosity or a noteworthy detail.

1.3 The Place of the Ketuvim within the Tanakh

An understanding of larger context is indispensable in determining plausible perspectives on any text. Therefore we must consider the role that the Ketuvim play within the context of Tanakh. First of all, it is necessary to note, especially for the Christian reader, that the Tanakh is not identical with the Christian Old Testament. Apart from matters of differing translation, some well known, the overriding fact is that of a pervasive difference in the organization of the Judaic and Christian canons of the Hebrew Scriptures. All Christian translations are based on the Septuagint, the original Greek translation mandated by the Hellenistic ruler of Egypt Ptolemy Philadelphus in the 3rd century BCE. The seventy ("septua") Alexandrian scholars who were required to produce the translation, in a Hellenized community out of touch with the main body of Jewry and destined for assimilation, endeavored to arrange the scriptural books in a quasi-historical order. A striking example of this is the placement of Ruth after the Book of Judges, on the grounds that the period of the Judges furnishes the setting for the Book of Ruth.

In definitive contrast to this stratagem, the Tanakh—canonized in the Babylonian capital of Jewish learning—organizes texts not quasi-historically but typologically, according to literary genre. Thus its first section is Torah, the supreme teaching of God revealed to the uniquely great prophet Moses; its second section is Nevi'im, the words and accounts of other major and minor prophetic leaders from Joshua through Malachi; its third section is the Ketuvim, considered to be non-prophetic miscellaneous writings by individuals working under the inspiration of the Spirit of Holiness, the *Ruach ha-Kodesh*, the least of three consecutive degrees of revelation that correspond to the three sections of Tanakh. Christians know the Ketuvim by the Greek term Hagiographa.

To appreciate the function of the Ketuvim intended by the Tanakh, we must consider the relationships among all three sections. Clearly, the heart of the Tanakh is the Covenant between Divinity and humanity enshrined in the Torah. This Divinity is not any deity but the Lord God whose identity is specified by His actions in the Torah and beyond; and the Covenant is confirmed not with humanity in general, as is the Covenant of Noah, but with the particular People of Israel—assigned to function as priest nation to others. From this core covenantal relationship, two inevitable extensions may be inferred and anticipated: one projects from the "Godward" side and the other from the "humanward" side. From God would have to come extended guidance occasioned by Israel's historical straying from covenantal precepts. This corrective guidance would be proffered by judges and prophets, successors to Moses who receive direct counsel from above.

On the other hand, the Covenant even if perfectly fulfilled does not offer answers to all of the searching questions that might arise in the free consciousness of a person committed to God's way. Answers to such questions could come only from human beings themselves, struggling to remain on the Divine path in the midst of many of life's gross and subtle, physical as well as spiritual, ordeals. These are the questions that the soul secretly asks itself, lying awake in the middle of the night. But adequate answers could crystallize only in the free reflections of humans inspired by the divine *Ruach ha-Kodesh*, the spirit of God. Thus as the Nevi'im embody "extended guidance" for Israelites from the "Godward" side, so do the Ketuvim embody "extended guidance" for these followers of God *from the "humanward" side* of individuals inspired by God. As we shall discover, authors of the Ketuvim raise the most penetrating, radical "boundary" questions that frame the human situation—some even challenging the Covenant. For freedom is the profoundest Divine signature and gift marking the human spirit, and only freely accepting answers to the most vexing questions of life is worthy of those made in the Divine image. Thus the guidance of the Ketuvim is every bit as needful as that of the Nevi'im in helping Israel to remain conscientiously, freely steadfast on its pained and protracted journey through history. In a sense, these texts find human freedom testing the Covenant itself in order that faithfulness to it might be firm and genuine.

Yet such guidance might not address Israel alone. The tradition of Israel has always had a place for non-Jews. Most intimately, a gentile could always join the family of Israel as a convert, never to be reminded of his or her non-Jewish origins. Abraham was instructed to circumcise, i.e., convert, all members of his household, and Ruth is considered the model convert. All gentiles dwelling in the Land of Israel were required to become "gerim toshavim," accepting minimal religious obligations. Fellow travelers or "God fearers" who embraced Judaic teaching but never "joined the family" were commonplace among Greco-Roman intellectuals; Aristotle interestingly called the Jews "a people of philosophers" and his student Alexander the Great to this day is recalled with warmth as a staunch friend of the

Jewish People. The Temple of Jerusalem was intended to be, according to Isaiah, a "house of prayer for all peoples." Finally, Judaism considers all humanity to be obligated by the seven Rabbinically-derived precepts of the Covenant of Noah, to be introduced to the world by the priest nation of Israel under the more demanding Covenant of Sinai. Today for the first time in history, a Noachide movement of thousands of mostly former Christians flourishes in the United States and elsewhere. Conversely, both Christianity and Islam have appended the Hebrew Scriptures to their small groups of sacred texts.

Rich historical precedent therefore exists for non-Jews finding spiritual nurture in the heritage of Israel. Precisely here lies the basis for the Ketuvim's encompassing message to all who believe in the One God of Abraham: living in regular obligatory relationship with the Creator, facing daily the spiritual tests produced by the Creation, all followers of Abraham confront similar trials on their journey of faith and may similarly profit from the guidance of the nine literary-theological texts of the Ketuvim. In these texts we may indeed discern the voice of Abrahamic monotheism at its most universal, embracing all who seek a path amid the variegated challenges encountered by humans as a part of Creation confronting the One Divine Creator. For Christians, finding new inspiration in the Hebrew Scriptures would come as no surprise. But Muslims, too, could find no objection to the universal Abrahamic spiritual wisdom of Ketuvim. For example, Islam regards both David and Solomon as prophets and Muslims in Iran venerate the Tomb of Esther.

The foregoing distinction between the Prophets and the Ketuvim also illumines why the Ketuvim include four books of a parochial, historical nature. Both the Prophets and the Ketuvim require groundings in Israelite history that reflect *their specific perspectives.* Thus the historical texts in the Prophets—Joshua, Judges, Samuel I/II, Kings I/II—reflect a perspective on the collective historical conduct of the People of Israel from the standpoint of Divine judgment. In contrast, the partially overlapping four historical Hagiographic texts offer a style of historical writing replete with moral and spiritual object lessens, appropriate to supporting and advising persons seeking truth and wisdom. To that search we now proceed.

— 2 —

Shir ha-Shirim: The Song of Songs The Theoretical Vision of Closeness to God

SCHOLARS have long speculated that *Shir ha-Shirim*, the Song of Songs, began its career as an erotic poem. Regardless, as heretofore noted, it was accepted into the Hebrew canon upon Rabbi Akiva's defense of the text as a profound allegory of the ideal love relationship between God and Israel. In Israel's stead, Christianity interpreted the text as the love between God and the Church. It is evident that Shir ha-Shirim could likewise be identified as a precursor to the Sufi poetry of Islam with its unitive mystical love.

Shir ha-Shirim has, to be sure, always been identified as an allegory. Its astonishingly erotic candor has, however, been a standing embarrassment to the pious, and the Judaic tradition has gone to great lengths to explicate and thereby minimize the allegorical surface. A fine example can be found in the Art Scroll Stone Edition of Torah and related readings. Here the translation bodily incorporates the muted interpretation of Rashi, the authoritative medieval commentator on Judaic sacred writings. Still, the vexing question remains: How to deal with the simple, surface meaning of this text? Must not the beautiful and evocative erotic poetry *itself* have a spiritual purpose that need not be explained away?

2.1 The Basic Theme

There is no need to analyze the text in detail in order to grasp its general dynamics. A profound bond exists between the king, understood to be *Sh'lomo*, Solomon, and a "black but comely" royal woman, taken to be the Queen of Sheba. Their relationship is characterized by a protracted mutual seeking of one another and a constant allusion to the beauty that each beholds in the other. There is reference to many often clandestine meetings and anguished partings. When separated, each is afflicted by anxious concern for the other and longs for reunion. Mysterious obstacles exist to the permanent union each desperately craves. Nonetheless their separations are mere transient episodes in a love that is "strong as death."

The woman is characterized as fairest of all. She is surrounded by the daughters of Jerusalem, who dote on her and seek to meet her concerns. She gives advice to them, who in turn both admire and envy her. Although many pine after the beauteous king, she is for him the only one. Their relationship is exclusive—by implication marital, whether in present or future.

2.2 The Marriage Metaphor

What has been called the "marriage metaphor" is, in fact, crucial to grasping Shir ha-Shirim. The theme of marriage recurs in several prophetic texts of the Tanakh. In *Hoshea* (Hosea), the prophet is required to marry a wanton women and bear children with this harlot wife, Gomer. That strange demand is for the sake of revealing to Hosea the agony that God goes through when his bride, Israel, consorts with others—whether through the "vertical" philandering of idolatry or the "horizontal" philandering of looking toward other earthly nations for protective alliances. Jeremiah begins by nostalgically reminiscing over how a faithful young Israel went after God into the wilderness as a bride of youth. Finally, Isaiah in Ch. 54 and thereafter celebrates the eventual true and permanent consummation of the marital bond, explicitly identifying God as bridegroom and Israel as bride. In later tradition, the Covenant of Sinai was likened to a marriage contract, the dedication of the wilderness Tabernacle was metaphorically identified as consummation of the marriage, and the Sabbath even now is seen as revealing the wedlock between Israel and the feminine Shekhinah (Divine Presence).

The marriage metaphor displays three levels of significance. First, recognizing the bond between the two principals in Shir ha-Shirim as *marital* is essential. Only marriage betokens a love so unbroken and deep that it weathers all disruptions, overcomes all challenges, spontaneously abides forever. Here, then, is the first level of the text's allegory: a depiction of the elemental character of the link between God and Israel as a relationship of the deepest, most ideal marital love. Here the message is that *marriage endures, the breaches will be overcome, the bond is indissoluble.*

2.3 The Deeper Significance of Marriage

But there is a deeper, second level to the allegory at which emerges the radicalness of this text and the boundary question it implicitly poses: *What makes an individual vulnerable to breaking solemn vows or a people to breaking sacred covenants?* It is succumbing to the pitfall of seeing the obligation as a matter only of *law* and not of *love*—of dutiful obedience rather than compelling attraction. Such a sense of burdensome law can make a relationship seem onerous and open the door to unfaithfulness. It prods the imagination to conceive of a fuller and more gratifying love experience than what one already has. This explains why Shir ha-Shirim is so openly erotic, presenting the lovers as fulfilling one another's deepest needs. The covert message is: *Everything you might be looking for is really here.* Thereby the text answers the radical, metacovenantal question "If I have deep needs, why should I not go where they can be fulfilled?" The response of the text to this question of profoundest yearning is: "Don't look elsewhere, delve *deeper* into your relationship with God. All the boundless love you crave lies in that relationship, and only there." This exemplifies a primary function of the Ketuvim—to address the most secret, radical questions of the spirit, which leave one open to using the gift of human freedom for going astray unless they are satisfactorily met. This second level clarifies *why* a true marriage is indissoluble.

Indeed, unless each adherent to the Covenant of Israel has the confidence that God's love will eventually satisfy the deepest yearnings of the whole person, how can any individual be kept from going astray? Thus the text deliberately portrays Divine love in ways that some might find scandalously erotic because it seeks to provide assurance that there is no corner of one's being that this love will not caress and minister to. It is *sheer love* that is crucial here, the craving of the whole human person to be fulfilled in every way. To ensure fidelity to the Covenant, it must promise no less than this—the complete satisfying of the human person. Because our impulsive yearnings easily tend toward the illicit, Scripture must affirm that no longing native to human body, heart and spirit will go wanting in and through faithfulness to the Covenant with God—our Creator knows and meets our needs. Such radicalness is ever fresh and startling; it cannot be outdated or superseded. This second level clarifies *why* a true marriage is indissoluble.

2.4 Law and Love Reconciled

But beyond even this assurance is an extraordinary third level of the marriage covenant: *reconciliation between law and love.* The significance of that resolution of tension is underscored by the fact that what is perhaps the most creative and profound theism of India, Bengal Vaishnavism, presupposes the supremely magnetic allure of extramarital youthful romance; it portrays the nakedly graphic erotic dalliance of the youthful all-attractive Krishna with the most exquisite of all the *gopis* (cowgirls), Radha. It endeavors to identify supreme love of God with adolescent illicit lustful amorousness, however elevated.

In radical contrast, Shir ha-Shirim affirms that in an ideal marriage the permanent contractual bond faithfully corresponds to and reflects a passionate love so deeply rooted as to be deathless—*permanent.* Thus *love* becomes the ideal content that *law*, as ideal form, holds, reflects and safeguards: *love and law merge and become one*—an insight that has implications for the entire Torah. Love is the true inwardness of law; law's purpose is to be fulfilled in and by love. The deepest of loves that did not wish to affirm and confirm itself in every way, including outward, publicly declared and noted eternal troth, would be a contradiction in terms. Content spontaneously seeks its authentic form. The profoundest love yearns to embody and explicitly proclaim its intention of absolute fidelity. On the other hand, lawful commitments that do not pave the way toward the total fulfillment of love can only be apprehended as a dutiful yoke and finally an intolerable burden. The only acceptable relational law is the law perceived to be that of one's *own innermost loving nature* impelled toward full actualization. This third level in the true meaning of marriage discloses an *organic connection* with the two other levels.

Shir ha-Shirim presents the Covenant as, in truth, an ideal marriage awaiting realization of its true identity and nature. Israel's deepest heart is that of passionate lover seeking fulfillment as youthful bride, eternally pursuing consummation with her Divine beloved. The ultimate reason that a total and perfect, passionate love must be marital is that it would not be perfect without including an open declaration of its nature and it would not be total without shaping not merely personal life but the whole context of social relations as only marriage does. True marriage is the only adequate expression of absolute love. Thus, as the theologian Abraham Joshua Heschel notes, *pathos* and *ethos* in God are identical and Israel is called upon to make them such in its own life with God. That is to say, true passionate love is in its deepest essence intrinsically ethical, incapable of intending harm to anyone, implicitly or explicitly, hence inherently "law-abiding."

Because Israel only learns gradually the depth of her own imbued love for and intended fidelity toward God, she strays and the path toward fulfillment is strewn with breakdowns and upheavals. Yet God remains ever faithful and separation is never confused with divorce. That is why Hosea is counseled never to divorce Gomer, however miserable he may become with her errant ways. Conversely, it is the love of Israel for God, no matter how inwardly buried for an extended time, that ensures she will ever return to His embrace—however heinous her outward strayings—until the return becomes permanent. The precondition of being the People of God is precisely such eternal fidelity, capable of withstanding all trials and all ordeals that might divert Israel in cleaving to the path of faithfulness. Jewish history is surely littered with such ordeals, all of them overcome.

2.5 Fidelity as Key to Israel's Survival

It is only this fidelity resulting in Israel's becoming the eternal people of history, preserved through every affliction by Divine Providence, that allows Israel's uncanny survival to function as *witness to the nations* of the reality of the Lord of history. *That* is the source of Israel's centrality in God's eyes. Ironically, it is only this faithfulness that will eventually inflect more deeply the relationship to the One God of all the other nations—the daughters of Jerusalem who would seem to represent the many nations, of whom they are princesses, included among Solomon's wives—and bring them, the nations, to fulfillment as well. Thus the daughters of Jerusalem, who understand this in the depths of their souls, attend upon the apple of Solomon's eye even while envying her. This is epitomized in the description "black but comely," an ambivalently racist allusion suggesting that the nations consciously perceive Israel in part as unenviably deficient—an unconscious denial?—although in the depths of their souls they recognize her virtues. Regardless, their own fate is bound up with hers. And only when king and queen have eluded the watchmen that intend to keep them apart, i.e., the wicked peoples that place obstacles between them, will the nations themselves—the "daughters of Jerusalem"—join the two in the eschatological celebration of a marriage completely fulfilled at last. Only thereby, communing fully with Israel and her One God, will they find their own destined spiritual flourishing.

— 3 —

Tehillim: Psalms

The Practical Handbook for Closeness to God

STRIKINGLY, Shir ha-Shirim presents "ideal relationship" not in a static but in a dynamic way, indeed in a historical way, reflecting Israelite scripture's emphasis on action and event. It does no less than disclose the *hidden inner history* unfolding within the outward scriptural saga of vicissitudes in the relationship between God and Israel. These vicissitudes are presented as expressions of the yearning struggle of two lovers to achieve their passionately desired union. In contrast, *Tehillim*, Psalms, is a practical handbook. It not only illustrates but provides actual language models for Israel's reaching out toward this ultimate closeness to God from any imaginable human situation—be it jubilant or sad, guilty or vindicated, pensive or engaged, fearful or triumphant, group or individual. As we shall see, the Psalms are far more than "prayers" although they include prayers.

Approaching the Psalms in a fresh way is somewhat daunting if one has been familiar with some of them since childhood. Nonetheless, only an openminded analytic reading can reveal their depth and unveil their spiritual indispensability. The sorts of question that must be asked are those typical of literary analysis, for example: Who is speaking? Who is being addressed? Is the voice individual or collective? Does the speaker change? What is the setting of the Psalm? What is the time orientation—past, present, future—and does it alter during the course of the text? Is the language involved or detached, descriptive or expressive? What is the spiritual and emotional mood of the Psalm? What are the sections into which the text can be divided and what is the nature of the movement from one to the next? Are the sections similar or different in their character, genre and tone? What is the spiritual aim and religious function of each Psalm? How can the text be incorporated into your personal life so as to become your own virtual language of address, aspiring toward greater closeness to God?

The best way to appreciate some of the variety and profundity of these extraordinary and unique texts is through analyzing a number of them. From these examples, the reader can develop approaches to other Psalms. The interpretations below require the student to have the text at hand.

3.1 Psalm 1

The first Psalm is uttered by an entirely impersonal narrative voice, noting a comparison between the natural and human/historical spheres. A person can desire and freely choose to search out the way of God and His instruction on which "he meditates day and night" (v. 2). He may be compared with a tree fortunate enough to be "deeply rooted alongside brooks of water. . . whose leaf never withers" (v. 3). Yet although water is a frequent metaphor for Torah, it is evident that unlike human beings the tree has no control over its location, e.g., near brooks. Still, as water is the necessary nurture for trees, so Torah freely chosen is the native and necessary nurture for the free human spirit. Accordingly, the wicked are "like the chaff that the wind drives away" (v. 4). Without firm moorings in their native spiritual environment, the wicked resemble dried plant materials that have become detached and are subject to involuntary banishment from the nurture of their natural soil. We are reminded that the rationally inferrable Author of nature (*Elohim*) is the revealed Lord of history (*Hashem*), and that the pursuit of Torah is natural law, inherent expression and highest fulfillment of the human spirit as Divine creation.

3.2 Psalm 19

But how may the Deity be approached through the readily available natural world in a way that confirms the identity of Elohim and Hashem—and establishes the truth that Personal Divinity is the only authentic aim for a human spiritual seeker? Consider vv. 1–10 of Psalm 19: These verses manifestly constitute a *meditation*: through v. 7 on the Deity as Elohim, Author of nature, and vv. 8–10 on the Deity as Hashem, Lord of history. "The heavens declare the glory of God. . . Day following day utters speech. . . [Yet] There is no speech and there are no words." This paradox is resolved by the realization that the *sheer existence* as well as order of the natural world, instead of the more "logical" absolute nothingness, implies and testifies to—"speaks" of—the glory of its Creator. As further example of that glory, the text continues with three verses describing the sun's magnificent and orderly cosmic movement. Then, in v. 8, "The Torah of the Lord is perfect, restoring the soul, the testimony of the Lord is trustworthy, making the simple one wise. . . ": The meditation has moved seamlessly from nature to historical revelation, observing that the same grandeur, perfection and order apparent in nature operates in divinely revealed instruction to humans—an instruction capable of bringing humans to their destined perfection. Just as the beauty and sublimity of nature can exalt the spirit, so "the orders of the Lord are upright, gladdening the heart; the command of the Lord is clear, enlightening the eyes (v. 9). . . The awe of the Lord (*Hashem*) is pure, enduring forever" as the physical Creation of God as Author of nature (*Elohim*) in its own way testifies (v. 10).

The next section of the Psalm (vv. 11–12) introduces the meditator as personally *appropriating* the truths he has been reflecting upon: "[The Lord's judgments] are more desirable than gold, than even much fine gold and sweeter than honey. . . Also when your servant is scrupulous in them, in observing them there is great reward." Now there follows a stunning half-verse transition to one and a half verses of intercessory *prayer* as the meditator realizes the full implications of his penetrating insights and the discomfiting reality of his human fallibility, which moves him to cry out in anguish: "Who can discern mistakes? Cleanse me from unperceived faults. Also from intentional sins, restrain your servant; let them not rule me, then I shall be perfect; and I will be cleansed of great transgression." The speaker is now motivated to aim freely in the historical sphere of his own life at the perfection that God has imbued in nature, but he has quickly recognized that only Divine help will suffice to achieve this. The final passage of the text (v. 14) explicitly and self-awarely acknowledges that what has been concluded is a *meditation*, personally appropriated and issuing forth in prayer: "May the expressions of my mouth and the thoughts of my heart find favor before you, O Lord, my Rock and my Redeemer." Here the author prayerfully hopes that his meditation has been worthy in God's sight.

Quite clearly, this text displays a complexity far beyond what we normally take to be "prayer." Studied closely, it is nothing less than a lesson in fruitful spiritual contemplation, whose efficacy is demonstrated when it spontaneously *issues in* prayer. We see that such meditation or contemplation is a process of seizing hold inwardly of truths that had formerly been mere abstract concepts. *Such is the very essence of monotheist contemplation.* So this modest text teaches a momentous and profound way to enter into the experienced presence of God. The Psalm must be embraced with one's whole being, and it will respond by deepening one's very capacity for spiritual perception and awareness. Furthermore, this Psalm illustrates that for the truly pious there is no gap between awareness of God and action. To become more deeply aware of Divinity *is* to turn toward It and reach for It. Any reflection on God that does not move one in this direction is vain and empty.

3.3 Psalm 23

But Divinity may be approached not only through the contemplation of *spatial* reality but of *temporal* as well. This most familiar of Psalms opens with a voice in distinct contrast to that of Psalm 19—whose initial timbre is that of an impersonal, anonymous recognition of the Creator's greatness as evidenced in things of space. For Psalm 23, the personal "I" is focal throughout. What changes is whom the Psalmist *addresses*. In the first three verses, the author addresses himself about God in a manner that emboldens his faith. Although he speaks in the present and even future tense, his faithful conviction conveyed by metaphors clearly rests upon an extended past personal history with God: "The Lord is my shepherd, I shall not want. He makes me to lie down in green pastures, He leads me beside the still waters. He restoreth my soul." In v. 4, the rhetorical object shifts more decisively from God to himself: "Yea, though I walk through the valley of the shadow of death, I will fear no evil. . . " Now his reflection shifts abruptly into prayerful affirmation as it directly addresses God: ". . . for Thou art with me." As in Psalm 19, reflections have brought him into the Divine Presence. Recalling God's faithfulness in the past, he affirms his confidence in God's care from the present into the future: "Thy rod and they staff, they comfort me, thou preparest a table before me in the presence of mine enemies," reiterating more deeply that with God—His guidance, discipline and care—he fears no evil. The text ends on a crescendo of confidently declaring an enduring faith that encompasses the totality of the speaker's earthly existence: "Surely goodness and mercy shall follow me all the days of my life, and I will dwell in the house of the Lord forever."

This Psalm thus falls into three distinct sections: (a) an initial affirmative reflection of the author addressed to himself, based upon recollection of God's past acts of goodness; (b) a direct present address to God, showing that the former reflection has ushered him into the Divine Presence here and now; (c) an affirmation that the God Who has always cared for him before shall—based on that evidence—surely care for him now and into the future. Whereas Psalm 19 starts from a contemplation of God's wonders in *space*, Psalm 23 opens with a recollection of God's faithfulness in *time*, successively treating past, present and future; nonetheless the speaker remains focused in the living present. Like the former psalm, Psalm 23 offers a spiritual lesson that one can enter into, showing how reflective gratitude for past Divine goodness lays the groundwork for trust in future beneficence. Once again, meditative reflection has led to faith's affirmation of God's abiding lovingkindness and care—and offered the reader a model to appropriate personally.

3.4 Psalm 37

The previous two Psalms were self-initiated meditations in which the Psalmist reaches out toward profounder relationship with God. But at times, God's faithful lack the inner fortitude to reach out on their own, requiring advice and encouragement. In Psalm 37 we find a personal voice instinct with spiritual wisdom addressing an individual in need of exhortation not to flag in the pursuit of truth and authentic relationship with God. This wise voice is of one who has manifestly achieved holiness and profound relationship with Divinity, conferring upon him a teaching authority to counsel others. The voice offers assurance to those navigating moments of doubt and weakness, needing support and guidance from someone farther along on the spiritual journey. The text is long, some 40 verses, and in the latter half the wise voice identifies itself with the personal pronoun in a famous passage: "I have been a youth and also aged; but I have not seen a righteous man forsaken nor his children begging for bread. . . Turn from evil and do good that you may dwell forever" (vv. 25, 27). A constantly repeated refrain is to rely upon and hope in the Lord, Who will soon defeat the wicked and save the righteous.

3.5 Psalm 70

In this short Psalm, we find a text typical of many in which the speaker is far from enjoying a placid contemplative mood, much less needing encouragement, but is rather in immediate existential crisis, turning to the Lord for rescue and deliverance: "O God, to rescue me; O Lord, to my assistance—hasten! Shamed and disgraced be those who seek my soul, repulsed and humiliated be those who desire my harm" (vv. 2–3)... "As for me, I am poor and destitute, O God, hasten to me!" (v. 6). This exemplifies the many texts that urgently petition a living and salvific God for redemption from concrete jeopardy. Here the reader finds an obvious paradigm for urgent petition.

3.6 Psalm 91

This famous Psalm opens with a human voice of affirmation: "I will say of the Lord, 'He is my refuge and my fortress, my God, I will trust in him'" (v. 2). It concludes with God's own voice explicitly responding, as it were, to the sort of cry embodied in Psalm 70, providing assurance that Divine rescue from distress is on the way (vv. 14–16): "For he has yearned for Me and I will deliver him... He will call upon Me and I will answer him... With long life will I satisfy him, and I will show him My salvation." The prior verses offer exultant reassurance of Divine protection: "A thousand may fall at your side and a myriad at your right hand, but to you it shall not approach" (v. 7). This voice leads the listener ever upward spiritually to arrive at the level of the angels: "He will charge His angels for you, to protect you in all your ways" (v. 11). And then in a transition as astonishing as it is seamlessly organic, the voice appears to reveal itself as having been the voice of God almost all along: "Upon the lion and the asp you will tread, you will trample the young lion and the serpent. For he has yearned for Me..." (vv. 13–14). This typifies the surprising shifts of person, temporality and mood with which the Psalms are replete, and the mysterious continuity between saintly and Divine voices.

3.7 Psalm 100

The salvation of the Lord must surely elicit gratitude from the redeemed, and Book Four of the Psalms overflows with psalms of praise, adoration and thanksgiving. Sometimes they definitively reach beyond Israel itself to portray Israel as priest people metaphorically urging the nations to join in acknowledging the One God. Typifying these is a short, exceedingly familiar text that illustrates Israel's role as priest people, in various ways used by God to draw the nations to Him. This psalm is unusual in that Israel's mandated priesthood does not actually include active proselytizing.

But here the collective voice of Israel exhorts the nations to acknowledge the Lord: "A psalm of thanksgiving, call out to the Lord, all the earth. Serve the Lord with gladness, come before Him with joyous song" (vv. 1–2). The need for such exhortation arises from the fact that although the Creator has made everything, the nations have yet to grasp and acknowledge this truth: "Know that the Lord, He is God; He made us and we are His, His people and the sheep of His pasture" (v. 3). Here is a remarkably universalistic passage, suggesting that God's people includes not only Israel but ultimately all His human children, all He has made, both those already aware of the fact and those not yet aware—as in Gen. 12:3, all the nations are intended to be blessed through the seed of Abraham with knowledge of the Creator. The text now issues its most explicit invitation for the nations to join Israel in worshiping the One God: "Enter into His gates with thanksgiving, His courts with praise; give thanks to Him, bless His name" (v. 4). Gratitude is evidently the key to entering the Divine Presence: from all creatures gratitude for their creation, intensified in Israel by gratitude for redemption from Egyptian bondage. The psalm concludes with a reaffirmation of the ultimate reason why the nations should welcome this invitation: "For the Lord is good, His kindness endures forever, and from generation to generation is His faithfulness" (v. 5).

These few examples do scant justice to the 150 individual Psalms of varying lengths and extremely diverse character. Virtually every imaginable human attitude that displays a potential motivation to reach out toward God is evident in these texts. All of life's situations find their voices in the Psalms. But all presuppose and are written within the context of relatedness to God, whether the Psalmist's mood is exalted or abject. Even moments of profound doubt, which the Psalms do not shrink from, are emplaced within the framework of ongoing relatedness to the Creator.

Embracing every life situation under the rubric of relationship with God highlights another lesson of the Psalms: *that there is no boundary between religion and life.* Every situation in life should be lived in the presence of and in relation to the Creator; God should be a partner in all one's experiences. It is this premise that makes the Psalms the practical handbook of what it means to live a religious life, which is nothing other than a fully *human* life, a life in which every moment presents an opportunity for drawing closer to one's Divine Parent. Although the Psalms have become a vital part of the liturgy in both synagogue and church, most of them are not collective hymns but personal declamations under the varied circumstances with which life confronts each person. No matter what you might be facing, so to say, you can find a Psalm that embodies the moment and places it in relation to God. Thus the Psalms teach how to relate to God *from any given concrete life situation.*

Following from this is yet another lesson of the Psalms: in them we find the absolute assurance that we *need never fear getting beyond God* since the Psalms include the feelings of doubt, of distance, of sin, of despair, of terror and show the reader how to reach back toward God's hand from any of these spiritual and emotional sinkholes. The Psalms display the full range of personal responses to life and God, including the most negative situations. Thus the Psalms teach how the human spirit may address God from any existential posture, how to talk with Him when feeling sad, lonely, sinful, heartbroken, betrayed. The Psalms appear intended for practical use, showing each person the words that need to be uttered in any given situation, until the words effectively become one's own voice—the voice of one's deepest spirit, liberated to address its Creator.

Finally, the Psalms reveal what it means to be a person dwelling moment by moment with the living God. In doing this, they disclose that in fact the only way *to BE fully a person is by living in relation to God.* Not to live in the presence of God is to be shut out of the fullness of life. Even by sharing one's despair with God, one demonstrates the empowering and reassuring confidence that someone is listening. And it is that very confidence that allows one to open up, express one's deepest realities and truly experience one's responses to life. To feel isolated is to become emotionally intimidated, numb and frozen, hence less than completely human. The Psalms offer nothing other than a portrait of the fully human and alive person who *is* so precisely because each moment is lived and shared with the Creator. Ultimately, then, the Psalms define a complete spectrum of personal ways of engaging with life and God, imparting to humanity that broad range of spiritual dispositions. Only when rooted in God may a person be truly open and vulnerable to others, entirely unafraid of abandonment and hence prepared to embrace completely and without anxiety the project of being human with all its varied facets.

— 4 —

Iyov: Job
The Theoretical Vision of Distance from God

HOWEVER much we need to understand how to draw close to God, we must equally master the shattering need to deal with Divine distance. As Scripture offers wisdom regarding closeness to God, so does it provide both a theoretical text and a practical handbook for coping with God's remoteness, often amounting to virtual absence. The theoretical text, *Iyov* or Job, is the Hebrew Scripture's closest approach to philosophy or philosophical theology, even paralleling Platonic or Upanishadic (Hindu) dialogues; these are found in the verbal interchanges between Job and his friends as well as between Job and God. Like any fine philosophy, the Book of Job poses many exacting interpretative issues to human intelligence, frequently approaching the enigmatic.

The text demands to be addressed with a large panoply of questions. For example: What is Job's interpretation of his problem; what is the essence of his complaint? How should we understand this problem in the context of the information we have about Job? What is the position of Job's friends? Are they to be understood as wicked, insofar as God rebukes them at the end of the tale? If not, how account for the rebuke? Is Job himself identified as wicked and, if so, why is he vindicated at the end? How does Job respond to his friends? What role does Elihu play? How shall we decipher the eventual Divine response to Job and Job's friends? Do these Divine responses seem adequate? What guidelines for human life in relation to

Creator and Creation does Job leave us with? Are the "prologue" and "epilogue" to Job probably later additions, as some scholars believe, or are they intrinsic and indispensable elements of the text? Is there any significance to the traditional idea that neither Job nor his friends are Israelites?

It may seem odd to refer to Job as presenting an "ideal portrait" of Divine distance insofar as "ideal" seems to connote something positive. In fact, it implies something more like "perfect form." And in Job, accordingly, we have an ultimate and in that sense ideal portrayal of absolute distance from God. First of all, we are informed that Job is the most righteous of humans and hence presumably merits the closest relationship with God. Yet what he receives is infinite woe, ranging from loss of children and property to personal physical affliction. This would seem to suggest ultimately severe, Divinely-inflicted punishment and, if it is not, why does Job undergo these ordeals? Adding to the intensity of Job's plight is the absolute refusal of God to provide Job with a hint as to why he is suffering. He also endures torment from his "friends" who try to persuade him that he must have sinned grievously for God to be so punitive and distant. Confronting the silence of God sprinkles the final salt in Job's wounds. Thus Job is the "ideal sufferer," modeling absolutely inexplicable, total distance from God in a way utterly irrational and unrationalizable by ordinary human religious logic.

4.1 The Prologue

Let us begin with the issues presented by the Prologue, Ch. 1, vv. 1–7. The first question is: Satan asks permission to test Job through imposing acute suffering. Are we to take this strange interaction between God and a very Hebrew Satan—i.e., simply an angel in the Divine court, assigned the special task of testing humans—literally? The answer can only be in the negative, because the central point later to be made in the body of the work is that humans *cannot* understand the ways of God, including events in His transcendent sphere. Why, then, this curious fable? If we discard the option of literal interpretation, it immediately becomes clear that the Prologue provides us with three essential inferences or data without which it is impossible to make sense of the text that follows. The first is that there is *some* sort of Divine reason for Job's suffering, even if it be beyond human comprehension: *that* is the purport of the fable's assertion that God has allowed Satan to test Job cruelly. The second vital piece of information is that Job, as he persistently asserts, is indeed blameless, the most perfectly righteous person on earth. This explicit assertion of the Prologue is equally necessary if we are to interpret the following text intelligibly. The third datum provided by the Prologue is a brutal, graphic description of Job's suffering—loss of his wealth, children and personal health. This confirms the stark contradiction between Job's spiritual and material conditions. To go beyond these preliminary bits of information into literal interpretation of God's dialogue with Satan would flout the most basic notion articulated in the text: that God's transcendent ways are not our ways and we cannot grasp them.

4.2 The Covenant Challenged

The body of the narrative begins in Ch. 2:9–11: "[Job's] wife said to him, 'Do you still maintain your integrity? Curse God and die!' Job said to her, 'You talk as any impious woman might talk. Furthermore, shall we accept the good from God and not accept the bad?' Despite everything, Job did not sin with his lips." This passage is one of the few in Hebrew Scriptures, another being in Isaiah 45, that clearly distinguishes Hebrew monotheism from Iranian dualism. For Israelite religion, there is only One Creator and the Creation is His alone—therefore all "evil" must somehow be traced back to God's permissive will, allowing errancy for the sake of human freedom even though God disapproves of wicked conduct and bemoans the evil consequences that He must providentially remedy.

In Job's response to his wife, the full radicalness of the text's central issue already emerges. *The ultimate test of covenant relationship with the One God is the temptation to surmise that He has failed to uphold the righteousness He Himself proclaims and has thereby broken His own covenant.* The Gnostics of the 2nd–3rd century CE succumbed to this very temptation and repudiated the Lord of history as an imposter deity. Similarly, Job's wife invites him to curse God for conduct that cannot be morally justified. But Job heroically deflects the temptation: "'Naked did I emerge from my mother's womb and naked shall I return there. The Lord has given and the Lord has taken away; blessed be the name of the Lord.' Despite all this, Job did not sin nor ascribe impropriety to God" (vv. 21–22). Nonetheless, Job's fidelity only deepens the perplexity of the situation. Job knows that neither he nor God is unrighteous—so why has he received evil from God's hand?

4.3 The Three Friends' Explanation

In Ch. 2:11, Job's three friends arrive on the scene to comfort him: Eliphaz, Bildad, and Zophar. Their motive is sincere—they weep, rend their garments and sit on the ground with Job for seven days and nights (the traditional Judaic *shivah* practice of grieving the death of close relatives). Respecting Job's anguish, they say not a word. Finally, in Ch. 3, Job pours out his agony verbally. Beginning with Eliphaz in Ch. 4, the friends respond. Their basic position flows from an assumption that such suffering *must* betoken Divine punishment. Therefore, sincerely believing themselves to be defending Divine justice, they infer that Job must have sinned: "Think now, who that was innocent ever perished. . . ?" (v. 7). The argument intensifies in vv. 17–19: "Can mortal man be righteous before God?...If he cannot have faith even in His servants and finds fault with His angels, then surely He does the same with those who dwell in clay houses. . . " Any creature endowed with free will, Eliphaz in effect asserts, must fall short of perfect Divine standards, so why foster the pretension that you're a unique exception? Moreover, the enormity of your suffering implies greatness of sin, since God apportions judgments by strict merit.

These three friends must be taken seriously. They are genuinely devout men, filled with compassion for Job yet believing they must defend Divine truth. Thus, according to their lights, they cannot concede that Job has been fully righteous. They believe that the only way they can help him is to convince him to repent. Job, however, responds to Eliphaz in Ch. 6: "Instruct me, and I shall be silent. Make me understand where I have erred... Empty talk is so much wind!...you dig a trap against your friend!" (vv. 24, 26). Job protests his innocence, but in Ch. 8, Bildad intensifies the indictment: "How long will you say such things? The words of your mouth are a powerful wind! Would God pervert justice? Would the Almighty pervert righteousness?" (vv. 2–3).

4.4 The Pivot of the Text

The following section, Ch. 9, requires scrupulous attention since it is pivotal to the Jobian conundrum. It begins with Job appearing to acknowledge the accusation of his friends: "Truly, I know that it is so. How can man be righteous with God? If he would want to contend with Him, He would not reply even once in a thousand. He is wise of heart and immensely strong. Who ever stubbornly opposed him and remained whole? (vv. 2–4)... If He would suddenly strike, who could restrain Him? (v. 12)... Could I, then, answer Him or choose to argue with Him? Even if I were right, I would not speak up, nor would I implore my Judge. (v. 14)... If it is for strength, behold He is mighty! But if it is for justice, who can plead on my behalf? Even if I am righteous, my mouth would condemn me. If I am innocent, it would pronounce me crooked. I am innocent, yet I cannot know rest!" (vv. 19–21).

Thus Job's real message is the *opposite* of concession to his friends. Rather, he testifies to the awesomeness of God's almighty power, shown in many ways. The particular mode that Job has in mind is hinted at by reference to *contending*, which first establishes the "courtroom metaphor" that later becomes more and more evident as the text unfolds. What Job is actually saying is that, supreme as He is in everything, God is also the supreme *prosecuting attorney*! A gifted attorney can twist the words of a defendant such that his own "mouth... condemns" him. Regardless of the innocence of the defendant, God's surpassless rhetorical skill could make Job seem in the wrong. And so it is that Job declares he is innocent despite all appearances to the contrary—despite his apparent punishment at God's hands. Contention with God is joined.

But now the text takes a strange and subtle turn, one pivotal to the remainder of Job's saga: "It is all one, therefore I say, 'He destroys both the blameless and the wicked.' When disaster brings sudden death, he mocks at the calamity of the innocent. The earth is given into the hands of the wicked; he covers the faces of its judges—if it is not he, who then is it?" (vv. 22–24). Only attentive analysis can expose the crucial tangent taken in these words. Is Job's first statement in the passage objectionable? Certainly not: it is a simple statement of fact. God surely destroys many of the wicked, as for example Egyptians at the Sea of Reeds, but he also occasionally destroys the innocent, as evident with Job himself. Given Job's strict monotheism, both good and evil are meted out by the One God—"if it is not he, who then is it?" But between these two impeccable statements comes something shockingly deviant: a vitriolic emotional indictment of God: "... he mocks at the calamity of the innocent." Is this statement justified as is the rest of the passage? The answer can only be emphatically in the negative. What Job has committed is the logical error of *generalizing from a single occurrence to an entire overarching pattern of vicious behavior.* From his individual inexplicable suffering, he has concluded that *it is a general disposition* of God to "mock... the innocent" sufferer. Carried away by his anguish, Job has inferred that he *understands* a universal mode of behavior of the one transcendent God. And here, as we shall see, he overreaches the realm of the permissible. Nonetheless, we shall be haunted until far into our deliberations with the question: has Job *sinned* or *erred*? Has he willfully defied Divinity or simply made an understandable and forgivable mistake?

Notwithstanding Job's implicit claim to understanding God's ways, his friends clearly transgress much more flagrantly. Job still refuses to affirm explicitly that God is unrighteous, although he has elevated to the level of principle that God destroys the blameless. Yet he backs into this conclusion reluctantly and without full awareness of what he has done. In stunning contrast, we now realize that Job's friends have felt entirely, brazenly assured that they understand God's ways as they confidently declare Job's suffering to be Divine rebuke. But does this unjustifiable though convinced assertion spring from a lack of piety? On the contrary, Job's friends accurately reflect the traditional piety of the Torah that asserts "If you adhere to the Covenant, I will bring the rain in its season..." And if drought occurs, conversely, you know you have sinned. Evidently what is on trial is *the traditional way of trying to grasp Torah itself*. Traditional religious logic, religious rationality with its straightforward sense of contradiction and the "excluded middle," has itself been fundamentally challenged. Torah's original principle of "as below, so above" stands in question. The compass has gone awry. What is going on?

4.5 Job Confronts God and His Friends

At the start of Ch. 10, Job's despair finally infuses him with the courage to confront God himself: "I loathe my life. I will give free utterance to my complaint; I will speak in the bitterness of my soul. I will say to God, Do not condemn me, let me know why you do contend against me. Does it seem good to you to oppress, to despise the work of your hands and favor the designs of the wicked?" (vv. 1–3). Here Job continues an ancient Hebrew scriptural tradition of challenging God that hearkens back to Abraham's debate with God over Sodom and Gomorrah. But now it is not two wicked cities but *religious rationality* itself that is in crisis.

After the third friend, Zophar, offers reiterated accusation of Job in Ch. 11, Job finally loses patience and gives vent to scornful contempt: "No doubt you are the people, and wisdom will die with you. But I have understanding as well as you; I am not inferior to you. Who does not know such things as these" (vv. 2–3). In Ch. 13, the "courtroom metaphor" comes fully into its own as Job makes his case against God while continuing his dismissal of his friends' contentions: "But I would speak to the Almighty, and I desire to argue my case with God. As for you, you whitewash with lies; worthless physicians are you all. Oh that you would keep silent, and it would be your wisdom!" (vv. 3–5). For silence would at least be an honest admission of incomprehension, which is what the situation truly demands.

There follows one of the most remarkable passages in the text in which the legal courtroom theme reaches its apogee: "Will you speak falsely for God and speak deceitfully for Him? Will you show partiality toward Him, will you plead the case for God? Will it be well with you when He searches you out? Or can you deceive him as one deceives a man? He will surely rebuke you if in secret you show partiality" (vv. 7–10). A fundamental principle of most legal codes, certainly including the Torah, is to show no partiality in judgment. A judge must be free of bias, incorruptible by bribes and unimpugnable in his integrity. Job is insisting that, as in a courtroom, a dispute is underway between him and God. If Job has convincing evidence against God, as he believes he has, God as just Judge will not be partial in rendering a verdict in Job's favor. If the friends take God's side simply out of bias or the attempt to curry favor rather than being guided by evidence, God will "rebuke" them—even if the partiality has been toward God Himself! Together with the legal disputations between God and Abraham and Moses, this is among the most penetrating examples of the "level playing field" which a Covenant establishes between God and humanity—and a precedent for later similar "lawsuits" in the Talmud. Job's seeming audacity confirms beyond doubt that what is on trial is nothing less than the "rules of the game" themselves as they have heretofore been understood. God no longer appears to be playing by the straightforward logic of reward and punishment, "as below, so above." The old rationality of the Covenant itself lies in shambles. What lies before us is an as yet *unprecedented crisis in religious understanding.*

In the remainder of Ch. 13, Job underscores the passion with which he pursues his defendant's sense of righteousness before the law of God: "Behold he will slay me; I have no hope. Yet I will defend my ways to his face" (vv. 15)... "Behold I have prepared my case; I know that I shall be vindicated. Who is there that will contend with me? For then I would be silent and die" (vv. 19–20). Job will continue defending his righteousness before God unless someone—God or another—proves him wrong, at which juncture he will be content to die.

As the chapters continue in grim procession, the motifs we have identified are reiterated many times with some elaboration. For example, in Ch. 19, Job sharpens his rebuke of the friends: "How long will you torment me, and break me in pieces with words... are you not ashamed to wrong me?" (vv. 2–3). His indictment of God likewise mounts in passion: "Behold, I cry out 'Violence!' but I am not answered; I call aloud, but there is no justice. He has walled up my way, so that I cannot pass... He has stripped from me my glory" (vv. 7–9).

4.6 Job's Integrity vs. His Friends' Indictment

In Ch. 27 we come upon another breathtaking example of Job's legal defense as he again responds to his friends' indictments: "As God lives, who has taken away my right, and the Almighty who has made my soul bitter; as long as my breath is in me; and the spirit of God is in my nostrils, my lips will not speak falsehood, and my tongue will not utter deceit. Far be it from me to say that you are right; till I die I will not put away my integrity from me" (vv. 2–5). For Job to admit the false claims of his friends would be to tell lies in court, as it were, and thereby traduce his righteous integrity, his sense of wholeness and self-respect—something that would contradict the core of his very identity. It is startlingly evident that Job will not compromise his integrity for the sake of humanity or *even God.* But it has become equally apparent that Job is convinced of his eventual "vindication," of Divine support for his case.

In Ch. 28, Job despairs of humans gaining access to wisdom: "But where shall wisdom be found? And where is the place of understanding? Man does not know the way to it, and it is not found in the land of the living" (vv. 12–13). As we shall see, this places Job's situation beyond even the radicalness of Ecclesiastes' view of wisdom; for Job, true wisdom (evidently understanding God's ways) is entirely inaccessible. And by Ch. 30, Job has lost all patience with the spurious "wisdom" of his friends: "But now they make sport of me, men who are younger than I, whose fathers I would have disdained to set with the dogs of my flock" (v. 1). He continues his bitter lament to God: "I cry to thee and thou dost not answer me; I stand and thou dost not heed me. . . " (v. 20). The next chapter concludes, "The words of Job are ended" (31:40).

4.7 Elihu's Testimony

Ch. 32 finds the words of Job's three friends ending as well: "So these three men ceased to answer Job, because he was righteous in his own eyes" (v. 1). Can this impasse be broken? We now hear for the first time a fourth voice, that of Elihu: "Then Elihu. . . became angry. . . He was angry at Job because he justified himself rather than God; he was angry also at Job's three friends because they had found no answer, although they had declared Job to be in the wrong. . . Now Elihu had waited to speak because they were older than he" (vv. 2–4). And he vows to show no "partiality" (v. 21) perhaps in contrast with the three friends.

For the first time in this text, we find Elihu complaining of Job's very questioning of God: "God is greater than man. Why do you contend against him, saying 'He will answer none of my words'? For God speaks in one way, and in two, though man does not perceive it. In a dream, in a vision of the night (vv. 12–15). . . Man is also chastened with pain upon his bed. . . then man prays to God, and he accepts him. . . " (vv. 19, 26).

This "second way" seems open to puzzlement, for it is exactly what Job has experienced and the repentance prescribed seems akin to the recommendations of Job's three friends—unless, of course, suffering is not in this case Divine chastening, a possibility that eludes even Elihu. Confusion regarding the purport of Elihu's message grows in Ch. 34: "... the wise man who hears me will say: 'Job speaks without knowledge, his words are without insight.' Would that Job were tried to the end, because he answers *like* wicked men. For he adds rebellion to his sin" (vv. 34–37). And at the end of Ch. 35: "Job opens his mouth in empty talk, he multiplies words without knowledge." On the one hand, the reiterated notion that Job speaks without knowledge resonates profoundly; on the other hand, we must wonder whether Job has actually sinned or just appears "like" the wicked. This ambiguity appears in the next chapter as well: "But you are full of the judgment *of* the wicked; judgment and justice seize you" (36:17). Is Job therefore actually wicked or just apparently so?

Then from Ch. 36:26 through Ch. 37, Elihu decisively shifts his focus to the greatness of God and our ignorance of His majestic ways as Creator: "Behold, God is great, and we know him not; the number of his years is unsearchable. For he draws up the drops of water, he distills his mist in rain..." (36:26–27): "Hear this, O Job; stop and consider the wondrous works of God. Do you know how God lays his command upon them and causes the lightning of his cloud to shine?" (37:14–15). Elihu concludes at the end of the chapter "The Almighty—we cannot find him... Therefore men fear him; he does not regard any who are wise in their own conceit" (vv. 23–24). The assertion that "we cannot find him" implies the utter transcendence of Creator over creature, however much His deeds and even Presence may be apparent on earth. As to those who are "wise in their own conceit," this surely includes the presumptuous certitude of Job's friends, but may it not also include Job's presumption that God is answerable to humans?

4.8 God's Answer from the Whirlwind

With Ch. 38, the final phase of the text commences and there is no doubt that God endorses and indeed echoes Elihu's affirmation that creatures cannot "know" Divinity in Its absolute transcendence: "Then the Lord answered Job out of the whirlwind: 'Who is this that darkens counsel by words without *knowledge*? Gird up your loins like a man, I will question you and you shall declare to me. Where were you when I laid the foundation of the earth? Tell me, if you have understanding. Who determined its measurements—surely you *know*!" (vv. 1–5). There is no mistaking the mocking sarcasm of the Divine Voice from the whirlwind, turning the tables to interrogate Job. The message is already transparently evident: How can a creature, incapable of grasping the most elementary realities of the Creation, presume to question the actions and decisions of an incomprehensibly greater Creator? The message is soon reiterated: "Have you comprehended the expanse of the earth? Declare if you *know* all this... Where is the way to the dwelling of light...? You *know*, for you were born then, and the number of your days is great!" (vv. 19–21). Job is being pummeled by an ironic and vehement Divine rebuke of his temerity in thinking that he could understand the ways of God. The reprimand intensifies in the next two chapters as the Voice continues to recount the many wonders, often taken for granted, of the natural world: "Do you *know* when the mountain goats bring forth? Do you observe the calving of the hinds... and do you *know* the time when they bring forth...?" (39:1–2). Finally, "And the Lord said to Job, 'Shall a faultfinder contend with the Almighty? He who argues with God let him answer it'" (40:1–2).

4.9 Job's Remorse

That Job has been accused by the supreme Prosecuting Attorney of audacity can no longer be at issue. What remains still obscured, however, is whether Job has sinned and is to be numbered among the wicked. The answer remains murky.

But at this point, Job takes a major step in ruing his audacity: "Behold, I am of small account, what shall I answer thee? I lay my hand on my mouth. I have spoken once, and I will not answer; twice, but I will proceed no further" (vv. 4–5). The Voice now reiterates its original indictment to drive home the point: "Gird up your loins like a man; I will question you, and you will declare to me. Will you even put me in the wrong? Will you condemn me that you may be justified?" (vv. 7–8). Thus God confirms Elihu's ire that Job has sought to justify himself rather than God. The rest of the chapter reprimands Job's self-assertiveness and then returns to recounting God's wondrous acts in nature, notably Behemoth, "the first of the works of God" (v. 19). Ch. 41 proceeds in a similar vein, devoting itself entirely to God's creative power evident in the greatest of sea creatures, Leviathan.

We have arrived at the final, remarkable Ch. 42 that, within a brief compass, solves all the riddles that Job has bequeathed to us. It begins with Job speaking: "I know that thou canst do all things, and that no purpose of thine can be thwarted. 'Who is this that hides counsel without knowledge?' Therefore I have uttered what I did not understand, things too wonderful for me, which I did not know. 'Hear, and I will speak; I will question you, and you declare to me.' I had heard of thee by the hearing of the ear, but now my eye sees thee; therefore I despise myself, and repent in dust and ashes" (vv. 2–6). Job receives no discursive answer to his questioning of God. What he does receive, however, is apparently an unprecedented nonverbal revelation of God's greatness as transcending the human capacity to understand Divine motives—what suffices Job is a vivid intuited reassurance that a just God, despite all earthly appearances to the contrary, remains in charge of human circumstance.

4.10 The Text's Central Issue

The profundity of this text now becomes inescapably manifest. No doubt Israel's original revelation disclosed a whole new sort of Deity, beyond paganism's mere personifications of determinative natural forces. This was a true *supernatural Person, free* to bring about harmony and justice rather than being compelled by nature's inherent physical characteristics with their inevitable conflictual aspects: the uniquely transcendent, unifying Creator of the universe. Nonetheless, the original revelations to Israel portrayed God as in some sense lawfully "predictable" and therefore at least analogous to the predictability of natural forces in their physical interaction. As surely as military conflict on earth signified political conflict within the council of Babylonian nature deities above, for example, so did drought on earth now evidently signify Divine displeasure above. *Yet from the outset, a Creator transcending nature was in principle not fully understandable by much less accountable to His natural creatures—His ways are not our ways.* At times, God might be constrained to take actions beyond our comprehension that might seem even to violate His own laws of justice. How was humanity to cope with such situations?

Only through a *new, deepened revelation* of God's fundamental incomprehensibility: the time had come to realize fully that we could know of Him only what He is able to disclose, while essential aspects of His nature and behavior *must remain inherently beyond our grasp.* This is clearly not because God willfully withholds information but because of creaturely incapacity to receive it. The Book of Job is the vehicle of this new revelation. Job *does* receive an answer from God, but not a discursive response to his questioning. Rather, he receives a new awareness of God's incomprehensibly transcendent greatness, symbolized by the theophany of the Whirlwind. This theophany, somehow directly experienced, reassures him that God truly exists in His incomprehensible transcendent greatness and may be trusted even though He eludes creaturely understanding. This is the "seeing" to which Job refers that brings a certitude far beyond ordinary intuition, teaching and so forth—likened to mere "hearing." Job therefore repents his projective creaturely presumption in thinking he could grasp God's motives.

4.11 Job Vindicated, the Text Illuminated

Job now receives that vindication from God that he was always confident would be forthcoming. The Voice addresses the three friends: "My wrath is kindled against [Eliphaz] and your two friends; for you have not spoken of me what is right, as my servant Job has" (v. 7). They are then instructed to offer sacrifice and request Job's prayers for their forgiveness, which God accepts. "And the Lord restored the fortunes of Job, when he had prayed for his friends; and the Lord gave Job twice as much as he had before" (v. 10). The Epilogue now depicts Job as comforted by his relatives "for all the evil that the Lord had brought upon him" (v. 11), and proceeds to detail the magnificent restoration of Job's possessions and children as well as his great length of days.

This extraordinary, succinct conclusion to the text ravels together most all the remaining loose threads of its message. These may be elaborated as follows: God's sense of justice, truth and goodness *does indeed* parallel our own and His historical design fully intends to realize these values in a way we will recognize, as Job's final restored fortunes illustrate and confirm. Nonetheless, the *way* that God pursues these ends is sometimes, if not often, beyond our comprehension. Still, we are not left rudderless in our creaturely quandary. We are girded with the outward word of Divine revelation and, sometimes even more vital, with the "still, small voice" within—the voice of our *integrity*, our wholeness, our spirit, our inner unity in which inheres the correctly guided intuition of the One in Whose image all human persons are made. In moments of uncertainty, the inner voice of conscience—the voice of spirit—*prevails. God firmly supports Job's conscientious integrity in defiance of his friends' remonstrations.* Our mission is to heed conscience and, assuredly, the external guidance of Divine commandment. But this Book unmistakably confirms also that we *cannot* assume suffering always betokens Divine punishment for breach of commandments, as Job resolutely insisted in the face of his friends' complaints.

Thus Job did *not* sin at all in questioning God—he merely *erred*, since the full majesty of Divine transcendence had not yet been revealed by the theophany of the Whirlwind. Job's bitter indictments of God are taken in stride as inevitable, given the hitherto prevailing understanding of Divinity as always acting in a humanly comprehensible manner. Job's friends, however, disdainfully ignored the challenge—issued by Job's conscience—to show him *how* he had erred, to specify concretely what he had done to merit such suffering if indeed it was Divine punishment. They could not meet this challenge, precisely because Job's suffering was indeed *not* punitive. Their cruelly glib arrogance, however well-meaning, properly invites Divine wrath, but their initial common ignorance—together with Job's—of the not yet revealed new theophany entitles them to pardon through Job's prayers; not wicked, the friends were merely conventionally pious.

4.12 The Final Questions

One crucial issue yet remains unaddressed. In the new, post-Jobian universe of uncertainty regarding the purport of historical events, in this now insecure world where what happens below does not necessarily reflect the Divine disposition above, how can a follower of God maintain basic faith and resist the claims that we, after all, dwell in a frigid universe ruled by sovereign chance, a chaotic world entirely indifferent to the welfare of human beings? Implicitly, the Voice from the Whirlwind addresses this enigma as well. Its message between the lines is: when the "book of history" becomes clouded and unintelligible, when the compass of historical meaning spins out of control, *take refuge in the "book of nature."* For the better part of five chapters, the Book of Job attends to the incomprehensible wonders of the natural world, confronting humans on all sides every day. Picking up on the testimony of Elihu, the Voice from the Whirlwind catalogues marvels of the Creation great and small whose essence eludes the grasp of creaturely intellect.

Beyond even these stands the seminal question of Abrahamic

monotheism: *Why is there something and not nothing?* Logically, "nothing" makes more sense. Who, then, is that Agent, that great *Someone* that must have had the will, the intelligence, the power and the freedom to *put* it all here? The *sheer existence* of the world is the most fundamental evidence of a Creator. And the bedrock upon which faith can stand when history loses its transparency is *nature itself*—the original, prehuman Creation. Knowing that we cannot even comprehend an ant within the created world, much less the *very existence of that world*, we regain humble perspective on our inability to grasp God's hidden dealings with the most elevated and grandest of His creatures—ourselves. Yet contemplating the world from the standpoint of radical monotheist insight, it becomes unimaginable that Someone, *God*, did *not* put it here, however humanly unfathomable His motives in history may have temporarily become. We continue to believe because we *must*, on the evidence of the sheer existence of the world itself, against all protests of limited creaturely rationality. And with that realization comes the Jobian fortitude to abide the concealment of the Divine Face until it eventually shines forth, illumining human history from beginning to end.

To take up our remaining preliminary questions, any doubt has been dispelled by their essential roles in our analysis that both the Prologue and Epilogue to the Book of Job are integral and indispensable components of the text. It is also evident that the tradition claiming no characters in Job are of Israelite origin implies that this message universally addresses *all* Abrahamic monotheists, grappling with the silence of God and how to reckon with it. Although such reckoning is painful, Job's theodicy—the technical term for reconciling an all-powerful, good God with the world's evil—has endured throughout the ages. Thus the Book of Job well merits its identification as ultimate theoretical text for dealing with the experience of absolute Divine distance.

— 5 —

Eicha: Lamentations
The Practical Handbook for Distance from God

THE Book of Job portrays an "ultimate" boundary situation in which God's silence and distance to the point of virtual absence cannot be explained through any trace of human failing—at least within human rational grasp. Consequently, there is nothing that Job can do to remedy the situation, other than wait patiently "upon the Lord" to set matters aright: the Book of Job teaches faithful acceptance of the incomprehensible. In contrast, Lamentations presents a situation of *fully* comprehensible total breakdown in relationship between God and human beings, in this case the Kingdom of Judah, that results from total human malfeasance, extended willful and heinous straying from the path of God.

Given this cause, remedying the situation lies entirely within the hands of human transgressors who face the practical task of somehow building a bridge back to relationship with the God Whom they have forsaken. Lamentations, however, also stands in fundamental contrast with its companion practical handbook—Psalms. In Psalms, no matter how bleak the mood may become including the bewailing of grievous sin, basic confidence endures that the relationship with God—however strained—remains intact. Only because of this confidence can the Psalmist freely pour out the sorrows of his heart to the Lord. In Lamentations, the bottom has fallen out of that intact relationship with the most excruciating consequences for human sinners. The connection to God has been utterly sundered, leaving survivors of Judah's calamity in bewildered consternation.

5.1 Complete Abandonment

What is depicted at the beginning of Eicha may without exaggeration be characterized as a holocaust. The axe has fallen—the worst has come to pass. The Babylonian enemy has not only ravaged Jerusalem and taken many of its inhabitants into exile, it has destroyed the very House of God, the Temple, the stronghold of the Covenant. No illusion, no hope remains that things might not be as bad as they appear. On the contrary, the people of Judah have hit bottom and undergone what they have every warrant to suppose is bitter, absolute rejection by God. Perhaps the most arresting exemplification of this is the text's image of mothers cannibalizing their own children out of desperate starvation. Such horror merits comparison with the Holocaust of our own times. The Face of God has become fully occluded. Here, then, is an ultimate boundary situation of total practical distance from God—practical both because it was occasioned by human misdeeds and also because only practice of the right sorts of action might possibly bring relief.

Traditionally ascribed to the prophet Jeremiah, Eicha offers internal evidence of thought and style suggesting that the same hand indeed authored the prophetic and the hagiographic text. From the first chapter, the prevailing theme of Lamentations is certainly lugubrious grieving over the horrendous fall of sinful Jerusalem. She sits alone, spurned, forsaken by God. The personified city speaks mournfully: "'For these things I weep; my eyes flow with tears; for a comforter is far from me, one to revive my courage...' Zion stretches out her hands, but there is none to comfort her; the Lord has commanded against Jacob that his neighbors should be his foes" (vv. 16–17).

Unlike Job, whom four friends attempt to console, Jerusalem is entirely abandoned. *If there is to be any recovery, it will have to come from within her shattered heart itself.* Unless hope can arise from the very ashes of despair, the career of Israel is finished. Jerusalem confesses her harlotry: "I called to my lovers but they deceived me... Behold, O Lord, for I am in distress... because I have been very rebellious" (vv. 19–20). Abandoned by her ostensible allies, Judah's remnant remains in total isolation. Ch. 2 confirms that the wrath of the Lord empowered the adversary: "The Lord has destroyed without mercy all the habitations of Jacob... He has burned like a flaming fire in Jacob, consuming all around" (vv. 2–3).

5.2 The Point of No Return

What was the point of no return at which the fate of the Kingdom of Judah was sealed? The clue appears without delay in Ch. 1: "Her uncleanness was in her skirts; she took *no thought* of her doom; therefore her fall is terrible... " (v. 9). She took "no thought" of her doom. When does return to an all-merciful God become impossible? *Only when the very possibility of such return has been forgotten.* Only then is the transgressor beyond help. Such forgetfulness is the price of continual, habituated wantonness that dispels awareness of God and the covenant relationship with Him into bottomless oblivion. At that point the sinner becomes incapable of considering the consequences of his or her willed actions. God has ceased to be a factor determining behavior. All deterrents have collapsed, allowing a headlong rush toward catastrophe. Judah, her heart hardened, was no longer *able* to take any thought of her doom.

5.3 Remembrance as Cure

To grasp that fatal *forgetfulness* was truly the turning point toward doom is to understand how a path of return can emerge from and indeed *only through* the very ashes of a despair that fosters *remembrance*. In Ch. 3, the parabola of anguish reaches its nadir and begins its ascent: "*Remember* my affliction and my bitterness, the wormwood and the gall! My soul continually thinks of it and is bowed down within me" (vv. 19–20). The Book of Jeremiah observes with seeming paradoxicality that in the disease is the cure. Here the meaning of that enigmatic claim becomes evident. If forgetfulness is the disease, remembering is the cure. And to be surrounded and weighed down to the breaking point by physical evidence of Judah's destruction is necessarily to "continually think of it," indeed to become obsessively preoccupied with it so as to be able to think of little else. That return of sustained thought produces the resurgence—perhaps re-engraving—of *memory*: Oh yes, there was a God with whom Judah had a Covenant, an intimate commitment which she trampled upon. And instantly upon the return of remembrance of God and the covenant follows the rebirth of hope: "But this I call to mind, and therefore I have hope" (v. 21). *For a God Who faithfully kept His covenantal promise to afflict can be relied upon to keep His covenantal promise to restore the penitent.*

5.4 Initial Recognition of Divine Faithfulness

This recognition of God's faithfulness to keep His word was already anticipated in Ch. 2 as part of the text's initial expression of anguish, before the realization that hope in the Lord is the other side of Divine destruction: "The Lord has done what He purposed, has carried out his threat; as he ordained long ago, He has demolished without pity... (v. 17). In Ch. 2, though, this realization occasions an almost accusatory high pitch of lament: "Cry aloud to the Lord, O daughter of Zion! Let tears stream down like a torrent day and night! Give yourself no rest, your eyes no respite! Pour out your heart like water before the presence of the Lord... Look, O Lord, and see! With whom hast thou dealt thus? Should women eat their offspring, the children of their tender care?" (vv. 18–20). Here lament is tinged with bitter indictment.

5.5 True Hope Inspired by Divine Faithfulness

Ch. 3, however, in its realization of hope in God's faithfulness to renew as the other side of God's faithfulness to destroy—Ch. 3 now abruptly shifts from despair to rhapsodic celebration; God's love will be as steadfast as the Divine rebuke has been unrelenting: "The steadfast love of the Lord never ceases, His mercies never come to an end; they are new every morning; great is thy faithfulness" (vv. 22–23). God's disposition toward His ruined people can become newly merciful the very next moment as penitence dawns. " 'The Lord is my portion,' says my soul, therefore I will hope in him" (v. 24).

5.6 Waiting as the Beginning of Return

A turning back to God (*teshuvah*) is now underway in good earnest. Lamentations at once proceeds to chart in detail the path of reversing the course of destruction. The first step is quiet, bittersweet *waiting*—waiting for the spirit of penitence thoroughly to permeate the people's soul as they wait for Divine salvation: "The Lord is good to those who wait for Him, to the soul that seeks Him. It is good that one should wait quietly for the salvation of the Lord. It is good for a man that he bear the yoke in his youth. Let him sit alone in silence when He has laid it on him; let him put his mouth in the dust—there may yet be hope; let him give his cheek to the smiter, and be filled with insults" (vv. 25–30).

It is as though the fallen sinner has become so habituated to the ways of wickedness that he must embrace a quietistic stance of inaction, anxious that any apparently innocuous move may be imbued with unconscious wickedness. At this stage, hope consists in a "hope for hope"—a hope of Divine cleansing and that a promising path of return to God may yet open up. The sincerity of this hoping for return can be demonstrated by nonresistance to those who would harm, absorbing their blows as a penitential sacrifice, an acknowledgment that one is deserving of such punishment and worse. But, most importantly, a new willingness to wait for the Lord demonstrates the rebirth of understanding and faithful assurance that God is *Lord of history* Who eventually will bring His purposes to pass. Although without immediate expectation, since there is no guarantee that God will act soon, the waiting is imbued with conviction that the Lord's compassion will eventually become historically manifest.

5.7 Faith in Divine Love Renewed

In this passive quiescence, the deep realization can grow that God's true essence is merciful love—that he allows affliction only when no alternative exists other than permitting wayward creatures to hurtle toward grievous destruction: "For the Lord will not cast off forever, but, though He cause grief, He will have compassion according to the abundance of His steadfast love; for He does not willingly afflict or grieve the sons of men" (vv. 31–33). God, as a loving parent, allows calamity to fall only as a last resort to save His wayward children, Who can no longer hear his guidance in any case. As the chapter continues (vv. 34–39), the speaker renews his awareness of past Divine righteousness and reconfirms the experienced faithfulness of God to keep His promises: "Who has commanded and it came to pass unless the Lord has ordained it? Is it not from the mouth of the Most High that good and evil come?" (vv. 37–38). Here is an echo of the crucial verse cited in Ch. 2 in which God's very act of destruction implicitly lays the foundation for faith in His promises of restoration: "The Lord has done what he purposed, has carried out his threat; as He ordained long ago, he has demolished without pity" (v. 17). We can now see that the final accusation sprang from an initial wild bitterness, for actually "in all their affliction He is afflicted." Thus strength and faith are indeed to be garnered *from the destruction itself* insofar as it proves God is reliable and trustworthy.

5.8 Soul-Reckoning while Waiting

The next step on the path of return can now emerge. While waiting quietly on a merciful Lord, there is something vital that may be actively undertaken: "Let us test and examine our ways, and return to the Lord! Let us lift up our hearts and hands to God in heaven: 'We have transgressed and rebelled and thou hast not forgiven"' (vv. 40–42). Such self-examination is known in Hebrew as *cheshbon ha-nefesh*, soul-reckoning, and is the primary task of the fall penitential season in Judaism. Probing the depths of one's dark failings elicits spontaneous confession of sin. Confession, when deep and real, can issue forth in deeper tears, not just of anguished lament but of conscientious remorse—a further step in returning: "My eyes flow with rivers of tears because of the destruction of the daughter of my people. My eyes will flow without ceasing, without respite, until the Lord from heaven looks down and sees..." (vv. 48–50). This weeping is fully cathartic, releasing deep pent up anguish of having undergone merciless destruction at the hands of Babylon. Such tears are profoundly healing.

5.9 Courage and Integrity Reappear

The start of healing now gives birth to a courageous clarity that feels secure enough to identify and take comfort from the fact that the People of Israel's enemies are far worse transgressors than Israel. The entire latter section of Ch. 3, from v. 52 to v. 66, anticipates the downfall of Judah's cruel adversaries: "Thou wilt requite them, O Lord, according to the work of their hands, thou wilt give them dullness of heart; thy curse will be on them, thou wilt pursue them in anger and destroy them from under thy heavens, O Lord." Isaiah confirms that the rising power of the Medes and Persians will indeed smite the arrogance of the Babylonians. And penitent Judah begins to recover the core of its integrity as God's committed servant among the nations.

5.10 Calm Retrospection and Reaffirmation

Most of Ch. 4 yields to the voice of grieving remembrance, but the lament now has the character of calm historical contemplation, culminating in v. 20: "The breath of our nostrils, the Lord's anointed, was taken in their pits, he of whom we said, 'Under his shadow we shall live among the nations.'" But the very next verse returns to the conviction that Israel's enemies, impelled by sin, shall be requited by God in turn: "Rejoice and be glad, O daughter of Edom, dweller in the land of Uz; but to you also the cup shall pass; you shall become drunk and strip yourselves bare" (v. 21). The chapter ends on a triumphant note of conviction that Israel will be restored even as her enemies are rebuked: "The punishment of your iniquity, O daughter of Zion, is accomplished, He will keep you in exile no longer, but your iniquity, O daughter of Edom, He will punish, He will uncover your sins" (v. 22). This assured confidence to indict Israel's tormentors transcends mere understandable vindictiveness: it acknowledges a realization that the worst has already befallen Israel, the ultimate pain of the nadir has been passed, and the remnant of Judah is now on the upward curve of return—unlike her tormentors.

5.11 A Trusting Plea of the Returnees

At the opening of Ch. 5, the last section of Lamentations, the theme of remembrance once more comes to the fore, but this time as an assertive yet implicitly hopeful plea to God—for Israel through Jeremiah again prays with tentative confidence as His People: "*Remember*, O Lord, what has befallen us; behold and see our disgrace! Our inheritance has been turned over to strangers, our homes to aliens. We have become orphans, fatherless; our mothers are like widows" (vv. 1–3). The plight of the people is ascribed primarily to the sins of their ancestors, whose burden they bear: "Our fathers sinned, and are no more; and we bear their iniquities" (v. 7). In vv. 8–18, a grim picture is painted of the current woeful condition of the survivors of Judah, enslaved by a victorious enemy. The section concludes by mentioning the theme of the sick heart, one which preoccupies Jeremiah and to a lesser degree Isaiah and Ezekiel: "For this our heart has become sick, for these things our eyes have grown dim, for Mount Zion which lies desolate; jackals prowl over it" (vv. 17–18).

The remarkable final passage of the Book of Lamentations begins by mixing a renewed awareness of God with the reality that the remnant of Judah still feels abandoned and forgotten: "But thou, O Lord, dost reign forever; thy throne endures to all generations. Why doest thou forget us forever, why doest thou so long forsake us?" (vv. 19–20). This last sentence about forgetfulness puts in poignant relief the chapter's initial plea that God remember His devastated people. But it is the next famous verse that bears the unmistakable imprint of Jeremiah and reveals the subtle logic of interplay between Divine will and human freedom that Jeremiah understood so well: "Return us to thyself, O Lord, that we may be returned! Renew our days as of old!" (v. 21)

5.12 The Logic of Jeremiah

The remnant of Judah now prays through Jeremiah for God to turn their heart toward Him, for only then will they be able to return. But the very fact of this prayer demonstrates that the turning and renewal of the heart is *already* well underway, otherwise the remnant would remain enmired in forgetfulness of God. But what produced that remembrance, giving rise to a prayer for Divine assistance in teshuvah, in returning? It was the very calamity of destruction that the text laments! The bitter but unmistakably authentic lesson is clear. When God has been utterly forgotten by free human beings, only nearly complete destruction can awaken remembrance. Yet this destruction is nothing but the direct consequence of forgetting and thereby abandoning God. Therefore the fact of a prayer for return being uttered shows that *the initial remembrance of God has already occurred, and God had already begun to answer the prayer through allowing—more accurately, being unable to prevent—the catastrophe that fostered remembrance.* As Jeremiah said, in the disease is the cure. When the disease of forgetfulness has run its course to the point of horrific destruction, the cure of remembrance is ineluctably born.

Here lies the grim secret of how return to God may be accomplished from the situation of an absolute collapse of relationship. The secret is hard, but unavoidable given the reality of God's commitment to human freedom made in the image of Divine freedom. The message is basically a universal one, applicable to the lives of all Abrahamic monotheists. But in the case of Israel, an additional level must be noted. The Song of Songs, together with prophets Hosea and Isaiah, make clear that although there may be many separations and breakdowns in the marital bond between God and Israel, there will never be a divorce since the Covenant is eternal. In the Book of Lamentations, we find the ultimate example of total disarray in the relationship, and discover how that very breakdown contains the seeds of recovery toward destined consummation of the marriage foreseen explicitly by Isaiah. Nonetheless, the seriousness of the crisis is underscored by the plaintive last verse of the text, revealing how fragile remains the confidence of Judah's remnant that true restoration of the bond will occur: "Or hast thou utterly rejected us? Art thou exceedingly angry with us?" (v. 22).

The fast of *Tisha b'Av* mourns the destruction of both temples and other calamities in Jewish history. It is of more than passing interest that the distinctive reading or *megillah* for that day, the last significant event of the liturgical year, is Eicha—this book that demonstrates the consequences of *forgetting* God; one of the very few other texts that may be studied on this fast day is Iyov. Tisha b'Av is the last significant religious occasion of the liturgical year. It is clear, then, why the first event of the *next* liturgical year, the New Year's festival of Rosh HaShanah, is called in the prayers for that day *Yom HaZikaron*—the Day of *Remembrance*. And in Islam, interestingly, the Sufi term for chanting the Names of God is *zikr*—remembrance.

— 6 —

Mishlei: Proverbs
The Practical Handbook for Maintaining Stability in Everyday Life

MISHLEI, the Book of Proverbs, radically shifts the focus of the Ketuvim from the "vertical" dimension of relation to the Creator to the "horizontal" dimension of relationship with the Creation. From the human standpoint, this largely entails relationship with human beings and human situations within the context of the Creation. The abiding focus, as the famous Ch. 8 will underscore, is on *wisdom*. Wisdom, as understood in the ancient Middle East and perhaps generally, is associated not with dicta handed down from a deity on high but rather with *experience* within the world, specifically with a sometimes painfully acquired awareness of how to meet and succeed at encountering life's challenges—routine but also extraordinary. The very word *mashal*, proverb, entails the notion of comparison. Wisdom is acquired by comparing the outcomes of different experiential approaches to life and seeing which ones are most effective.

The Book of Proverbs is often associated with ascribed author Solomon's middle life as he teaches to his son what he has learned about what works in the "school of life". The authorial voice is that of someone who has discovered through his own hardwon experience the truths about how the world of human creation actually functions. Thus wisdom is in its very essence *practical*. The fruit of experience, i.e., wisdom, is discovery through the experiment of daily living what prevails and what fails to succeed in the real world. It is thus an experiential encounter with the *lawfulness inherent in Creation.* The subject of this text is the actual, concrete way in which human experience operates, proved through living day by day in the world as it is given to us by the Creator. The author is one who has paid attention, who has cultivated awareness of outcomes as human beings interact at home, in the marketplace and elsewhere and as they seek to find the most constructive behaviors and uses of their time and energy. The implicit boundary question is: *How can we conduct our lives so as to conform with the lawfulness inherent in Creation and thereby live in the world as successfully as possible?*

6.1 Starting with the Awe of the Lord

In both Ch. 1:7 and Ch. 9:10, the start of acquiring wisdom is clearly identified: "*Reishit chokhma yirat Hashem*"—The beginning of wisdom is the awe of the Lord. The word *yirah*, often translated "fear," may be illumined by its sonic resemblance to *re'iyah* "seeing." The implication is that to see clearly and thus correctly Who the Creator is results in a natural feeling of awe for His greatness. And, of course, the correlate of this is to recognize the world as Creation. This includes a sense of my true status in the scheme of things. Thus the intuition of *yirat Hashem* surely entails humility but not craven humiliation—rather the natural, not at all undignified humility felt by a being in the presence of another Who is manifestly greater. This is not a paralyzing feeling of self-effacement but rather a galvanizing awareness of what truly is the foundation of the world and hence of one's own existence and experience.

6.2 Awe as Condition for Experiential Learning

But, more exactly, why does learning from experience in the *world* start with awe of the *Lord*? Quite simply, if you become aware that you have a Creator, certain inferences necessarily follow. To realize that you were created entails that the Creator had a *reason* in mind for your existence. This implies both that there is a destined place for you in the scheme of things—in the world as humans know it—and that you are *accountable* to the Creator to seek that niche. There must be some way of life that accords with His purpose for me, and I am beholden to find that way. If I fail to live in accordance with the Creator's design, my life will become difficult and burdensome. Stating the point positively, to know that there is a Creator elicits a frame of mind that allows me to live my life in the knowledge that there is One to Whom I am accountable for my actions. In this manner, the awe of the Lord orients me to the world of experience so as to perceive it as a *school* within which I will gradually come to discern the inherent lawful order that the Creator has established as the foundation of Creation. Only now can my experience in the world be directed productively instead of being as hazardous as it is haphazard. And only now do I have an opportunity to discover my unique place within the Creation's lawful order.

6.3 How Awe Enables Wisdom

But precisely how, then, do I begin *actually to find* that underlying order within Creation and human experience specifically that will lead me to the realization of my purpose for being, to the unique fulfillment that the Creator intends for me? The first step is disclosed in Ch. 30, vv. 7–9:

> Two things have I asked of thee; deny me them not before I die.
> Remove far from me falsehood and lies; give me neither poverty nor riches;
> Feed me with my allotted bread; lest I be full, and deny and say "Who is the Lord?"
> Or lest I be poor, and steal, and profane the name of my God.

Here in Mishlei is the famous *via media*, or middle way, that profound thinkers in cultures around the world have discerned in one fashion or another. In this case, the author seeks a happy medium between riches and poverty to avert the danger of losing sight of God—resulting in an essentially false view of life. Should he be too poor, he may forget God in his overwhelming suffering and feel impelled to steal. On the other hand, an excess of riches can lead to prideful arrogance and the sense that one has no need for God. This via media thus has as its objective nothing other than *continuously remembering the reality of God*; for only then can yirat Hashem remain the foundation of one's life and the portal of wisdom remain open. The message is: *do whatever is required to keep your focus on God.* For if you forget the Creator and lose awareness of your accountability to him, the trapdoor of folly will open. Conversely, so long as you keep the Creator in full view, your behavior will be infused with wisdom. Only thus will you be able to see human life, including your own, in proper perspective, make sense of things, come to true judgments about human circumstances. For example, you will understand that even if the sinner appears to prosper, he will eventually fall since he is failing to live in accordance with the inherent lawfulness of Creation, which includes human nature. So even if the sinner seems to be enjoying a more gratifying life, you will not envy his transient pleasures: "Let not your heart envy sinners; surely there is a future." In this way does wisdom begin to emerge from experience.

6.4 The Future

Remembrance of *the future*, then, flows directly from yirat Hashem and is a basic facet of wisdom. This remembrance is a vital aid in overcoming temptation to sin. For to sin is to ensure a dark and painful future. Temptation can assume subtle forms: "There is a way that seems right but leads to death"—be on guard against lethal shortcuts to the future that God intends. Even if you do not yet understand God's purpose for you, "surely there is a future" in which that purpose will be realized if you cleave to yirat Hashem. The motivation to maintain a lively hope for that future of fulfillment is the determined remembrance of God, His goodness, His perhaps as yet unfathomed purpose for creating you. Sometimes we have glimpses of the fulfillment that might be ours, but it seems unattainable or too distant. Through keeping one's focus on the Creator, we will be strengthened to take the long view, see our lives in totality as He does—and thereby resist succumbing to an undermining temptation: "Yirat Hashem is a fountain of life" (14:27).

6.5 Prudence

Clearly, keeping life in its true, largest perspective of your creatureliness will lead to your intuitive grasp of wise choices, sane living, good outcomes. *For there exists a natural lawfulness in Creation that may be grasped even without revealed commandments.* Once this grasping is underway, you will see and embrace the value of *prudence*, since it constitutes a fundamental key to the *via media* of Proverbs. Prudence entails making life choices based upon a longrange view of circumstances and outcomes. The prudence that arises in the perspective of wisdom will allow you to see with a clear immediacy the foolishness of experimenting with fleeting pleasures of the moment, such as drugs and wantonness, that lead to prolonged anguish and pain. It will be evident to you that succumbing to transient temptations will upset your life's long-term balance—hence are not in your true interest. It is noteworthy that however much yirat Hashem is the beginning of wisdom, then, the focus of this text is not on cultivating a relationship with the Creator but on living wisely within the Creation. But to that end, remembering the Creator is indispensable.

6.6 Experience as Instruction in Wisdom

Thus can all your life experience become *instruction*—so long as you cleave to the perspective of wisdom, which is nothing more nor less than perpetual, living awareness of the Creator. Building upon the fundamentals of the reality of the Creator, the consciousness of your accountability as creature, and your need to safeguard these twin pillars of wisdom, you will understand ever more deeply how to plan and live your life wisely so that it will bring true satisfaction and fulfillment. It should come as no surprise, then, that the bulk of the Book of Proverbs consists of specific nuggets of wisdom expressing in manifold concrete contexts dicta rooted in the foundations of wisdom. All of them are entirely clear and virtually self-evident so long as you maintain the perspective of wisdom. All of these exemplary precepts encourage you to manage your life with healthy caution, apprehending it as a totality, accountable to the Creator. Don't embrace momentary pleasures that will undermine fidelity to your true larger interests. Aim at enduring, nurturing human relationships rather than fleeting exchanges with strangers. Recognize that certain behaviors will fructify in permanent happiness, others in lasting misery. All these realizations and more come to those who seek the instruction of wisdom that Mishlei mandates: "It is the glory of God to conceal things, but the glory of kings to search them out." This apparent contradiction is resolved in the recognition that what God truly conceals and what humans are encouraged to "search out" are not the same. For the Israelite worldview, humans are active copartners with God in completing the creation and the legitimate search for wisdom—for experience as infused with "instruction"—exemplifies divinely intended human participation in understanding the basis for the good life.

6.7 Experiential Wisdom Proves God's Word

Mishlei's middle way entails an apparent vital circularity. Whereas the awe of the Lord is the beginning of experiential wisdom, experience in turn validates the words of the Lord: "Every word of God proves true" (30:5). Here the emphasis on practical experience returns. The claim of the text is that experience, when consulted honestly, will prove God is right and His words are reliable. Thus we may infer that although the "awe of the Lord is the beginning of wisdom," the awe of the Lord is *not* the beginning of experience. Rather one *arrives* at yirat Hashem through experiences in the school of life, through experiments with living that both succeed and fail. Some persons require great suffering to encounter the reality of the Creator. Genuine awe of the Lord is not given at the beginning of life but arises at some point in the unfolding of one's existence. Before then, we may have been going astray or we may have been behaving virtuously but without true understanding of why virtue is virtuous. But when we attain to yirat Hashem and can begin to develop wisdom, we will be in a position to recognize with full existential appreciation how experience bears out and proves God's word to be true.

Thus Mishlei implicitly envisions the sequence of a proper human life. One begins without a real apprehension of the Creator. Human freedom confers upon us the privilege to learn by trial and error, making life a series of experiments. Eventually, whether along a high road of virtue or a low road of error, we encounter experientially the reality of the Creator to Whom the only possible authentic response is awe—*yirat Hashem*. Having found this reality, we become determined not to lose sight of it, for to do so would be to wander aimlessly back into the thickets of chance—to place ourselves at the mercy of random circumstance. The very measures we take to maintain a focus on the reality of the Creator naturally turn our experiences into instruction in right living—which is righteous and successful living. This instruction gleaned from the course of a human experience that deliberately remains attuned to God, the Creator, is the very essence of *wisdom*. Once we have grasped existentially the foundations of wisdom, we can most profitably study its details set forth in Mishlei. These details furnish wise guidelines for many particular conditions and situations arising in everyday experience. As we grow in wisdom, we develop a profound, internalized understanding of life—both strategies to meet its challenges as well as pitfalls to strategically avoid.

6.8 The Role of Discipline

In the vision of Mishlei, perhaps the most important outgrowth and adjunct of wisdom is *discipline*. The text dwells often upon self-discipline, the disciplining of one's children, the discipline taught by life that is virtually equivalent to wisdom. As wisdom is to intellectual understanding, so discipline is to behavior: "Whoever loves discipline loves knowledge" (12:1). Wisdom, a creature of experience, is fragile and can be lost unless it is applied. Discipline is *applied wisdom*. Discipline takes the body in hand and trains it and its behavioral reflexes to adhere to the path illumined by wisdom. Thus one can gain through experience the wisdom to avoid sloth or the attractions of wantonness. But without turning such wisdom into disciplined behavioral precepts, one can slip—for the ways of folly are easy and its blandishments tempting. Forgetfulness ever lurks at the door. Virtue, in contrast, develops only through disciplined effort, and one becomes willing to exert the effort only when wisdom has illumined and inspired the understanding.

Wisdom recognizes that self-indulgence is a folly leading to self-destruction, rather than to the happiness it deceptively promises, but only firm discipline can hold powerful temptations to indulgence at bay. Discipline, especially when imposed on children, may be painful at first and evoke resistance, but its necessity will eventually be appreciated; for discipline reflects the most basic perception of wisdom that our children will one day, we hope, also realize for themselves: in the long run we will find ourselves having to render accounts for our behavior, both in the fruits of a life lived well or ill as well as before our Creator. Most important, perhaps, only wisdom leads to a truly happy, fulfilling life.

6.9 In Praise of Wisdom

In the unique and remarkable Ch. 8 of Mishlei, Wisdom is personified and speaks for herself (*Chokhmah*—Wisdom—in Hebrew is feminine): "The Lord made me as the beginning of His way, the first of His works of old. I was set up from everlasting, from the beginning. . . When there were no depths, I was brought forth; when there were no fountains abounding with water, before the hills was I brought forth" (8:22–25). One can easily see why the Rabbinic tradition would often identify Wisdom with Torah, described in similar terms. This would pave the way for later mystical tradition to identify the "woman of valor," to whom the last Ch. 31 of Mishlei is devoted, with the feminine Shekhinah, the Divine Presence—especially since this aspect of Divinity, also called Malkhut or Sovereignty, is the only one to relate directly to Creation. Insofar as Wisdom emphatically constitutes the innate natural order of things, there might also be an interesting comparison with the Chinese Tao—which emphatically stresses a middle way.

In context, there is no doubt that all the discrete proverbs and sayings elsewhere in this Book are to be taken as pronouncements of Wisdom. Wisdom as an entity, poetic or otherwise, constitutes the platform upon which the entirety of Mishlei stands. And this very fact introduces a theoretical issue of sufficient purport to require another book to clarify it adequately: *Kohelet* or Ecclesiastes, treating the theoretical basis for maintaining stability in everyday life.

— 7 —

Kohelet: Ecclesiastes The Theoretical Basis for Maintaining Stability in Everyday Life

KOHELET bears the stigma of being considered the most pessimistic text in the Tanakh. Even the Rabbis indicated that it was included only because of its last line, recommending yirat Hashem. But, as we shall see, not only is this far from the truth—as the indispensable companion book to Mishlei, the two complement and illumine one another so as to deliver comprehensive counsel for dealing with the ordinary, stable regularity of everyday life. What makes Kohelet the theoretical companion to Mishlei is that it tests the premise upon which all of ishlei is founded: *the nature and primacy of wisdom as source of practical guidance for life.* This Book daringly raises the question of whether the very quest for wisdom may be misguided and whether the outcome of such a quest might be fraudulent. It asks whether it is possible for wisdom itself to be unwise. Standing above Mishlei on a plane of lofty philosophic scrutiny and analytic relentlessness, it probes and interrogates the very foundational assumptions of Proverbs: *Granted that Mishlei asserts the primacy of wisdom as practical guide, how can we be truly certain that what we take to be wisdom actually is?* Without a satisfactory answer to this question, the edifice of Mishlei rests on sand.

Most commentators find in Kohelet the voice of an aged King Solomon, one who has ventured down every avenue of experience to see what treasures or disappointments it might yield. He has done it all. The underlying premise is: you need not redo the research of this wisest of people. By investigating what makes for worthwhile living, he has done the work *for* you. In so doing, he has arrived at the highest wisdom to answer a crucial boundary question: *how do I find ultimate satisfaction in life?*

7.1 An Emphasis on Vanity

An immediate objection to the above claims might be that the text mentions wisdom only secondarily. That is true enough. Instead, it is intensely preoccupied with what constitutes an *opposite* to wisdom—vanity or folly. The Hebrew word *hevel* with which the Book opens might connote both senses of the English word "vanity"—preoccupation with the self and its presumed refinements; and *futility*—an effort that is in vain. The reputed dourness of this text springs from its blanket pronouncement that "all is hevel." Everywhere people, driven by vain preoccupation with the self, pursue a futile search for self-gratification: surely a good definition of folly. And everywhere such activity is *hevel hevalim*—vanity of vanities. Everywhere such activity brings no solace, so people—evidently in Solomon's time as today—seek out novelty, something new that might bring the longed for fulfillment. But nothing does, for "there is nothing new under the sun" (1:9).

7.2 A King's Despair

Ch. 1 goes on to paint a grim portrait of a world of endless cycles, all of nature toiling without end or lasting gain. This may be Israel's closest approach to the Indo-European pessimism of Indian or Greek cyclic time. In Ch. 2, the author declares his kingship over Israel: "And I applied my heart to seek and to search out by wisdom concerning all things that are done under heaven. . . and, behold, all is vanity and a striving after wind." But the author's apparent derogation of wisdom has only begun: "Lo, I have gotten great wisdom, more also than all that were before me over Jerusalem; yea, my heart has had great experience of wisdom and knowledge. And I applied my heart to know wisdom, and to know madness and folly—I perceived that this also was a striving after wind. For in much wisdom is much vexation; and he that increases knowledge increases sorrow" (2:16–18). Apparently, then, striving for wisdom is no less a folly than any other pursuit. The king then extends his quest for something worthwhile to encompass mirth, material pleasures and grand works, riches, lavish amusements—nothing was beyond the reach of this monarch. His conclusion? "For of the wise man, even as of the fool, there is no remembrance forever; seeing that in the days to come all will long ago have been forgotten. And how must the wise man die even as the fool! So I hated life. . . " (2:16–17).

7.3 A Curious Reversal

Pessimism indeed, or so it would seem! But a curious reversal of tone insinuates itself at the beginning of the very next, very famous Ch. 3, prepared for by a surprisingly positive view of temporal cycle at the very end of the previous chapter:

> To every thing there is a season and a time to every purpose under heaven:
> A time to be born, and a time to die;
> A time to plant, and a time to pluck up that which is planted;
> A time to kill and a time to heal. . .
> A time to love and a time to hate;
> A time for war and a time for peace. . . (3:1–8)
>
> [God] has made everything beautiful in its time; also he has set the world in the. . . heart, yet so that man cannot find out the work that God has done from the beginning even to the end.
> I know that there is nothing better for them than to rejoice, and to get pleasure so long as they live. . . (3:11–12)

> ...Wherefore I perceived that there is nothing better than that [a man] should rejoice in his works; for that is his portion; for who shall bring him to see what shall be after him? (3:22).

In Ch. 3, the king deals with the *identical cyclic aspect* of Creation that he regards so despondently in Ch. 1—but here, he finds "everything beautiful in its time!" Again, in the first two chapters Solomon seems to approach omniscience in his mastery of wisdom, claiming to have searched out "all things that are done under heaven," yet here he humbly confesses that "man cannot find out the work that God has done... " Moreover, whereas Solomon's initial searching finds wisdom a "vexation," Mishlei extols it as the indubitable foundation of Creation and Solomon speaks respectfully of wisdom later in Kohelet. A radical shift of attitude has evidently occurred. Yet the only distinction seems to be that Ch. 1–2 treated natural phenomena and Ch. 3 human phenomena. Wherein lies the real difference? Perhaps the clue is that *God is not mentioned at all* in the text until the end of Ch. 2: "There is nothing better for a man than that he should eat and drink, and make his soul enjoy pleasure for his labor. This also I saw, that it is from the hand of God...For to the man that is good in His sight He gives wisdom, and knowledge and joy... " (2:24–26). Here is the Deity's debut, along with a new view of wisdom as a Divine gift.

7.4 Reconciling Proud Despair and Humble Acceptance

Evidently the "wisdom" of which Solomon boasted in most of the first two chapters was not the wisdom celebrated in Mishlei as *beginning* with the awe of the Lord, yirat Hashem. Rather this must have been a "wisdom" that Solomon pursued in the same way as he later pursued mirth, palaces, riches and the like. But all these other possessions were merely baubles fancied by a monarchical ego—and proved, indeed, to be hevel. Then we are driven to the ironic conclusion that, no doubt because of his greatness in the eyes of others, *Solomon himself* lost sight of God for a time and pursued "wisdom" as just another commodity which a powerful, exalted and wealthy person might seek to gain in order to try to fill his or her interior emptiness. Perhaps that is why his investigation begins with the grand sublimity of nature rather than with the homely truths of human life. It seems that the king in his grandeur for a time was full of himself rather than full of devoted attention to God, believing anything that might be possessed—including wisdom—was his for the taking as were his reputed thousand wives. Thus as Kohelet opens, an undoubtedly younger Solomon himself exemplifies the very vanity he decries!

The devastating proof of his initial egoistic self-involvement is that the final straw bringing him bitterly to "hate life" was the fact that he, the renowned "wise king," would *die* and be forgotten like any mere fool. Chafing at one's mortality is hardly a mark of wisdom, but of youthful arrogance. No wonder the self-centered Solomon of the first two chapters, clinging fiercely to his foreordained physical finitude, would find everything hevel, "wisdom" included. Yet already, at the end of Ch. 2 and in 3:22, we have seen him edging away from this pouting despair, saying "... for who shall bring him to see what shall be after him?" Here is a new humility that admits death may or may not be the end, but we cannot know. We have no choice but to infer that the king has now progressed considerably on the road of life experience toward a more discerning grasp of reality. Unfortunately, the text gives no indication of any passage of time. Nonetheless without assuming a substantial temporal transition between Ch. 2 and Ch. 3, perhaps from middle age to sage elder, the text becomes unintelligible.

7.5 Confirmation from the King

A shocking surmise, perhaps, but an inescapable one. Thus it is not really surprising that the text itself eventually confirms dramatic change in the king's own view of wisdom—as well as recognition of his own vanity: "All things have I seen in the days of my vanity" (7:15)... "All this have I tried by wisdom; I said: 'I will get wisdom'; but it was far from me. That which is is far off, and exceeding deep; who can find it out. . . ?" (7:23–24). The last phrase confirms that the voice is that of the later humbled Solomon. Finally the king entirely repudiates the "wisdom" he at first thought he had mastered: "When I applied my heart to know wisdom. . . then I beheld all the works of God, that man cannot find out the work that is done under the sun. . . yea further, though a wise man think to know it, yet shall he not be able to find it" (8:16–17).

7.6 Rejoicing in One's Portion

But we have already seen hints of a more sanguine theme appearing in Solomon's reflections as early as the end of Ch. 2: "I said in my heart: 'The righteous and the wicked God will judge; for there is a time there for every purpose and for every work'" (3:17). "Behold that which I have seen: it is good, yea it is comely for one to eat and to drink, and to enjoy pleasure for all his labor. . . for this is his portion" (6:17). "Every man also to whom God has given riches and wealth, and has given him power to eat thereof, and to take his portion, and to rejoice in his labor—this is the gift of God" (6:18). . . "So I commanded mirth, that a man has no better thing under the sun, than to eat, and to drink and to be merry, and that this should accompany him in his labor all the days of his life which God has given him under the sun" (8:15). . . "Enjoy life with the wife whom thou lovest all the days of the life of thy vanity, which He has given thee under the sun, all the days of thy vanity; for that is thy portion in life. . . " (9:9).

These passages suggest that each person has a "portion" in life, his or her divinely intended place in the world, a destined spouse, a niche that may vary in terms of wealth, power, and fame. Yet it is only in that niche that each can find the designated "portion" in life that will be the source of his or her "rejoicing"—his or her true happiness. This is fully consonant with the Tanakh's prevailing view of reality. In the Israelite worldview, the universe is a unified whole consisting of unique yet interdependent, equally indispensable parts. Each part, whether great or small, makes its necessary contribution to the whole. And a part achieves its true identity and fulfillment only in finding its appropriate place within the whole.

7.7 The Source of Hevel

On the other hand, human "parts," endowed as they are with freedom, can misperceive themselves as freefloating atomized individuals with no sense of a destiny within some whole. Fulfillment for them becomes a futile and empty quest for that genuine satisfaction that can only be found when one has found his or her true, interrelated niche *within* the whole. Thus *any* motivation whatsoever that springs from the alienated individual ego is hevel—whether it be directed toward riches and pleasure or piety and wisdom—whether it be engendered by commoner or king. The search will inevitably end with a lonely descent into futility and even despair. For no person in *himself* possesses the principle of the *meaning* of his or her own existence: that meaning is discerned only in finding one's authentic "portion" within the whole of humankind, one's true place in the whole of Creation.

We can now understand one of the most enigmatic passages in this text: "Be not righteous overmuch; neither make yourself overwise; why should you destroy yourself?" Here the king touches on the subtle ensnarement that can taint a genuine quest for wisdom and righteousness and turn it into a self-aggrandizing pursuit of ego enhancement. In the light of Mishlei, we may infer that when the focus shifts perhaps imperceptibly from God to "wisdom" or "righteousness," when the goal of remaining attuned to the Creator is displaced by an *outcom of* or a *means to* that goal, then truth has been perverted and the soul is in peril. *Thus the test of true wisdom is whether or not it genuinely springs from yirat Hashem or from the ego, however ingeniously disguised.* It goes without saying that many egoistic ventures in ostensible pursuit of wisdom, righteousness and other virtues are not disguised at all.

7.8 *Kohelet* and *Mishlei*

Having recognized this, we can go on to discover any number of passages in Kohelet which resonate with the wisdom of Mishlei. Here, for example, are words reminiscent of Mishlei's stress on remembering the future: "It is better to go to the house of mourning than to go to the house of feasting; for that is the end of all men...The heart of the wise is in the house of mourning; but the heart of fools is in the house of mirth" (7:2, 4). Yet this mindless frivolity is clearly not the same "mirth" that Solomon enjoins in Ch. 8:15 above—the mirth of one who has found, accepted and is rejoicing in his portion. The latter is one who "fears God," an injunction repeated several times in the text before the final, famed admonition to yirat Hashem—awe of God. Closely related to remembrance of the future is remembrance of God, a recurrent theme in the Ketuvim, including Mishlei and Kohelet: "Remember...your Creator in the days of your youth, before the evil days come and the years draw nigh when you shall say, 'I have no pleasure in them'" (12:1). All this brings us full circle to the issue of penetrating definitively the message of Kohelet.

7.9 The Message of Kohelet

First of all, study of this text disperses decisively any aura of supposed pessimism. Kohelet is indeed pessimistic, but only about the *prospects for the self-involved ego ever finding satisfaction.* Neither can this ego ever find the wisdom or righteousness or happiness it believes it seeks. The problem is its steadfast alienation from the whole of Creation wherein alone it can find the true niche that will bring fulfillment. It goes without saying that the self-involved ego has not yet found true yirat Hashem either: one cannot find the Creator without finding the wholeness of Creation, and vice versa.

On the other hand, the frustrations of Solomon's egoistic quest have brought him to a contrary embrace of humility before the Lord that verges on religious existentialism. He certainly advocates yirat Hashem and affirms a "beautiful" Divine order evident in the Creation, but appears to have given up altogether on understanding God and His concealed purposes whether within human life or beyond it. He confesses to ignorance regarding human fate after death. But he resoundingly affirms the basic Israelite worldview with respect to the part finding its true identity and fulfillment only within its designated whole. It may be debated whether his attitude is fatalistic regarding locating one's own true niche. Does one simply accept circumstances as the will of God? Or must one search both inside and outside for clues as to where one belongs within the Creation? Since the evidence that a true niche has been found is being able to "rejoice in one's labor," perhaps the latter is closer to the truth. Regardless, the simple conclusion of the text is that cultivating deliberate enjoyment of your life—for however long you're granted it—is the only wise response to a universe whose Divine mysteries remain impenetrable and which would otherwise is fraught mostly with sorrow. This admonition is not far from the message of Zen, existentialism and other minimalistic approaches to life that take the world as it is moment to moment without extraneous assumptions. It need hardly be mentioned that such enjoyment must be consonant with the familiar conclusion to the text: "... fear God and keep His commandments" (12:13); it is certainly consonant with life affirmation amid suffering, a constant feature of Israel's religion.

Kohelet, in sum, could be said to demonstrate the *limits of wisdom*: on the one hand, the spurious wisdom of the empty, alienated ego seeking to gratify itself—on the other hand, the zealous spirituality seeking to overextend wisdom toward the "secret things" of God where, unlike mysticism perhaps, it is not equipped to go. As much true wisdom, Solomon ultimately finds a "middle way," a *via media*. This wisdom whose outer boundaries are clarified by Kohelet, and whose inner contents are exemplified in Mishlei, is freely available to every human soul seeking to make its way through a world fashioned by a Creator Who does not leave those made in His image devoid of guidance ready to hand. Surely Ecclesiastes demonstrates with extraordinary depth the nature of wisdom. It confirms the message of Proverbs by showing, as Proverbs cannot, *why* true wisdom is what it is, exposing the danger of counterfeits. In a word, true wisdom can be recognized in that it begins with humble awareness of the Creator and the corollary realization that any person's task is to find the "portion" designated by that Creator for him or her within the Creation. Any other sort of "quest for wisdom" has its roots in the folly of alienated, empty, ultimately despondent isolated ego. Kohelet's profoundly penetrating and timeless grasp, undergirding Mishlei, sets on a firm footing of genuine wisdom and perhaps even "meta-wisdom" the task of coping with the daunting challenges of ordinary daily life.

— 8 —

Rut and *Ester*: Ruth and Esther The Practical Handbooks for Dealing with Disruptive Change in Life

Our analysis has arrived at the fourth and final pole of our schematic chart: dealing with disruptive change in Creation. For people this generally entails human situations in the context of the created world. Without proceeding any farther, it is worth taking a moment to marvel at what remains before us. First of all, we must seek places uniquely for *three* books within the *two* categories of practical and theoretical. But, lest we lose heart, we note the astonishing commonality among these books even before we undertake to reflect upon them. Ruth, Esther and Daniel are all *tales, narratives, stories named after their protagonists.* Each heroine or hero encounters a *disruptive change* that radically alters her or his life and instigates a crisis or crises that must be dealt with. In each book, God is conspicuous for His virtual absence as a "visible" character although His providence is evident. In other words, a generic affinity—statistically highly unlikely—embraces the three texts that just happen to remain unexamined after the conclusion of our preceding analyses. And the common theme just happens to be exactly what our structural outline prefigures: *disruptive change in human life.*

As we approach the end of our Ketuvim texts, some history of the development of the structural schema is worth recalling from our Introduction. First, the hypothesis that the most basic polarity within Creation is "stability and change" was derived from its prevalence in ancient non-Israelite philosophical systems—*not* from any examination of Ketuvim texts. Secondly, the decision as to which category would have to accommodate two books was made on the basis of elementary literary analysis that sought an obvious pairing. That obvious pairing linked Ruth and Esther as "practical handbooks," leaving open the question as to why two books are uniquely required for this one out of eight schematic slots. Thirdly, the author—like most honest students of Hebrew Scriptures—was both relatively unfamiliar with and totally mystified by Daniel. This strange text, laden with apocalyptic visions that provide Sunday morning radio preachers with an endless supply of speculative material, nonetheless had only one category left to assign to it: the *theoretical basis for dealing with disruptive change.* Since no time remained to check out this association, the author had to plug it into his class syllabus in desperate hope that Daniel could be made to fit its assigned slot. The reader will soon enough have an opportunity to judge whether this fit is forced or inescapable.

8.1 Comparisons and Contrasts

Not much literary scrutiny is required to discover that Ruth and Esther could not be more of a pair if they were written by the same author with that deliberate intent in mind. Let us first note similarities between the two since discerning likenesses is less problematic than accounting for differences. It is obvious that both protagonists are women, and noteworthy that in many religions, Judaism included, the *spirit* is considered feminine. Both women have crises—one individual, the other public—that result in a radical change of situation, physical environment and status. Both changed situations result in intermarriage between gentile (or former gentile) and Jew: Ruth, the ethnic Moabite, marries wealthy Boaz and Esther marries Ahasuerus, the King of Persia. Intermarriage in each case embeds the heroine in a royal lineage. God is not mentioned in either book, but is intensely present in the form of providential intervention. Both stories end in happy vindication of the heroine's efforts.

In terms of contrasts, a simple beginning is to note that whereas Ruth is motivated by *mercy*—love for Naomi, her Israelite mother-in-law, Esther is motivated by *justice*—the need to thwart the evil scheme of Haman, the king's adviser, to annihilate the Jewish People. Mercy and justice are, of course, the basic moral attributes of both Divine and human persons in scriptural tradition. Ruth acts voluntarily out of heroic and courageous devotion whereas Esther is nudged into her public role of heroic and courageous exposure to peril by her uncle Mordechai, leader of the Jewish People—who is, indeed, the first biblical figure to be designated "Jew," a person from Judea, Yehuda. Ruth is initially poor whereas Esther, as a leader's niece, must have been a person of some means.

8.2 A Contrast in Types of Crisis

But the key contrast between the two, leading toward profounder insight and an understanding of why two texts are needed for this category, involves *the type of crisis* each heroine confronts. Esther's crisis is huge, public and short-term with a definite beginning and a definite end: Haman seeks the end of the Jewish People and his machinations are thwarted. True enough, Jewish tradition sees Haman, like Hitler, to be descended from Amalek, Israel's archetypal enemy in the Torah, but once Amalek is defeated, the skirmish in an ongoing conflict ends at least for that episode.

Now what of Ruth's crisis? It is surely the opposite of Esther's in that it involves the seemingly inconsequential personal decision of a devoted, loyally loving Moabitess—with no apparent bearing on historical events, unlike Esther's adventure in the Persian king's palace. But Ruth's circumstances bear much closer inspection. If Esther's crisis is short-term, what may be said of Ruth's crisis of decision? What is the time frame within which this decision discloses its full consequences? Consider first Ruth's ultimate origin. Who was Moab? Moab was a people descended from one of the two daughters of Lot who, witnessing the incineration of Sodom and Gomorrah, concluded that they were the last people on earth left alive. In order to propagate the human race, they therefore made their father drunk and copulated with him. Each had a son by their father Lot, Ammon and Moab ("from a father") respectively. This apparently repugnant incest must, in fact, be judged generously. The daughters sought no pleasure but were rather impelled by the virtuous motive of *saving the human race* as a physical entity. That they were misguided in their assumptions does not sully the purity of their motive.

So much for Ruth's origins. What of her destiny? Through her marriage to Boaz, Ruth became the great-grandmother of King David. But far more was involved in this marital bond. The initial breach within the family of Abraham was between Abraham and his nephew Lot, whose herdsmen quarreled over pasturage. Thus each retinue went its separate way. In the marriage of Boaz and Ruth, this first of several breaches in the Abrahamic lineage was in principle forever healed! In principle, one might even say that the rift between Jew and gentile was overcome. Moreover, the descendants of David would have the admixture of a gentile bloodline entwined with their Israelite genetic inheritance. Now David, according to tradition, would become the forefather of the *Mashiach*, the anointed leader who centuries later would lead the world into the Final Redemption, making peace between Israel and the gentile nations. Evidently his partly gentile heritage going back to Ruth and Boaz would facilitate this reconciliation. The Mashiach, then, would save the entire human race in the full and proper way, ushering in an era of universal peace, justice and prosperity.

Then the time frame within whose context Ruth's seemingly inconsequential personal decision must be understood extends from the generation of Lot, which is the time of Abraham, up to the generation of Mashiach ben David, Messiah son of David—*all of Israelite history*! And this vast expanse of historical time is thematically connected by the notion of *saving the human race*, which Ruth's ancestress attempted improperly and Ruth's descendant would accomplish in the full and rightful way; indeed, Ruth's own motive was not to abandon—and thus to help save—her beloved relative. The obscured context for situating Ruth's decision is therefore as *long-term* as the Israelite tradition allows, in contrast with the *short-term* public context of Esther's role in an immediate salvation of the Jewish People from a clear and present threat. Whereas Esther's action saved the Jewish People in an open and obvious way, Ruth's action would eventually save all humankind together with Israel in a manner still being patiently worked out by a concealed Providence. What initially appeared to be an inconsequential personal decision, then, turns out to be *a watershed for all of human history*.

8.3 Why Two Books?

At last it becomes evident why dealing with disruptive change requires *two* practical handbooks. We can now discern that the polar contrast between Esther's challenge and Ruth's challenge define a *spectrum* along which any sort of variant crisis precipitated by disruptive change could be placed. There simply is no way this reality could be represented except through having two contrasting texts as termini implying innumerable concrete possibilities lying between them. Pondering this spectrum invites one crucial spiritual observation: Some challenges are obviously, publicly momentous as was the case with Esther's. But even the most apparently insignificant personal decision today could, like Ruth's, be a linchpin from which the larger destiny of the world is suspended. Therefore *no* decision may be presumed inconsequential, and every decision demands the fullest spiritual, intellectual and moral weighing. Having noted the critical difference between the two heroines and their tales, this observation finally invites a return to their common ground. This will become apparent as we inquire into what these two books recommend as a response to crisis and challenge, wherever it may fall on the vast spectrum our two texts delineate.

8.4 Responding to Crisis and Challenge

The response our books envision to crisis is basically the same and essentially quite simple. Two elements are required. First, the better the spiritual character of the individual facing a crisis, the better equipped he or she will be to confront it. In both Ruth and Esther, we have models of virtue, courage, loyalty, selflessness, and so forth. For those of us less well endowed, the implied prescription is to summon up all our spiritual resources and training, proceeding in prayerful caution to determine our course of action. Secondly and most importantly, both texts are striking in that—despite His apparent absence—God maneuvers indispensably behind the scenes by means of His *hashgacha*, His Providential intervention in human affairs which often appears to be "coincidence." Esther in particular is a model of Divine Providence standing behind virtually every critical occurrence in the narrative. But the long arm of Providence frequently manages Ruth's affairs as well. Therefore the second requirement in responding to a crisis caused by disruptive change is strong faith in the active workings of Divine Providence, supported by whatever prayerful outreach one feels inspired to make. One must know that God is in charge and His intentions are always for the good.

But how may this crucial faith in Divine Providence be maintained at the requisite strength to face the unpredictable crises that life flings in our path? For this, we must explore the theoretical basis for dealing with disruptive change.

— 9 —

Daniel: Daniel
The Theoretical Basis for Dealing with Disruptive Change in Life

DANIEL is the culmination of our study of the Ketuvim, and it is fitting that the journey we have taken and the clues gathered from other books help prepare us to unravel the mysteries of this baffling text. Most of its main points may be gleaned from the first six chapters. Six final chapters offer a startling and totally unexpected confirmation of those main points. This tale is set in the Babylonian court of King Nebuchadnezzar, conqueror of Judah who left the devastation portrayed in Lamentations.

9.1 The Narrative

Daniel is among several captive Judaean youths of exceptional talent that the king has brought into his court for special education and cultivation. Daniel immediately demonstrates his faithfulness to God by successfully beseeching his appointed overseers to allow him not to consume the king's defiling food and wine. To each of four outstanding and similarly pious youths God gives a special talent—to Daniel, "understanding in all dreams and visions" (1:17).

"And in the second year of the reign of Nebuchadnezzar, Nebuchadnezzar dreamed dreams; and his spirit was troubled, and his sleep broke from him" (2:1). The king demands of his sorcerers that they make known to him both the dream and the interpretation—an impossible task, with the result that the king ordered all the wise men in the realm to be slain. This included Daniel and his friends, who all prayed for Divine intervention: Daniel received the king's secret "in a vision of the night...

> Blessed be the name of God
> From everlasting even unto everlasting;
> For wisdom and might are His;
> And He *changes the times and the seasons*;
> He removes kings and sets up kings..." (2:19–21)

Thus the text introduces early and explicitly the theme of an *ultimate source of change*, both orderly, stable change as with the seasons and disruptive change as with the overthrow of kings.

Daniel now appeals to Arioch, appointed destroyer of Babylon's wise men, to spare the wise men and bring him, Daniel, to the king where he would declare the interpretation. Daniel begins by giving credit for knowing the dream and its interpretation to "a God in heaven that reveals secrets" (2:28). Thus the important theme of hidden knowledge is introduced. After describing the king's dream, Daniel again testifies regarding God: "Thou, O king, king of kings, unto whom the God of heaven hath given the kingdom, the power and the strength, and the glory..." (2:37). He goes on to interpret further that the king's dream images refer to three kingdoms after Nebuchadnezzar's, each inferior to its predecessor, until finally God will establish a kingdom that "shall stand forever" (2:44). "Then the king...fell upon his face, and worshipped Daniel...and said: 'of a truth it is, that your God is the God of gods, and the Lord of Kings, and a revealer of secrets...'...Then the king made Daniel great and made him to rule over the whole province of Babylon..." (2:46–48). Here parallels with the Joseph narrative are unmistakable.

Nebuchadnezzar then fashions a golden image, presumably representing Daniel's God, and demands that at a signal everyone will fall down to worship it or else be cast into a fiery furnace. Daniel's three friends refuse and declare that even if their God is unable to deliver them from the furnace, they will worship none of Nebuchadnezzar's gods. When they emerge unscathed from the fire, Nebuchadnezzar decrees that none may speak ill of the three nor of their uniquely salvific God. The three receive honors and promotions, and Nebuchadnezzar praises God throughout his realm.

For almost the first half of Ch. 4, Nebuchadnezzar is speaking. Once again, he has a troubling dream and once again calls in his sorcerers to interpret it. Only Daniel, however, is able to do so. What he sees frightens Daniel, but the king bids him speak: ". . . this is the interpretation, O king, and it is the decree of the Most High, which is come upon my lord the king, that thou shalt be driven from men and thy dwelling shall be with the beasts of the field. . . till thou know that the Most High ruleth in the kingdom of men, and giveth it to whomsoever He will..." (4:21–22). A disruptive change indeed, apparently intended as a cure for an idolatry reminiscent of the Golden Calf. All this comes to pass a year later, announced by a heavenly voice. Eventually "at the end of the days" (4:31), Nebuchadnezzar truly blesses and praises God, and his kingdom is restored to him.

The next chapter abruptly shifts into the future, depicting the king's son and heir, Belshazzar, making a great feast using golden vessels taken from the Jerusalem Temple, all the while honoring Babylon's idols. A mysterious hand writes upon the plastered wall, and the frightened monarch calls in his sorcerers and astrologers who cannot read the writing. The queen remembers Daniel, who is summoned. Daniel reminds Belshazzar that God heaped greatness upon his father until Nebuchadnezzar grew proud and God had to humble him until he "knew that God Most High ruleth in the kingdom of men, and that he setteth up over it whomsoever He will" (5:21). Knowing all this, Belshazzar nonetheless had defiantly staged his blasphemous banquet. Having delivered his admonition to the king, Daniel interprets the writing: "MENE, God has numbered your kingdom and brought it to an end. TEKEL, you are weighed in the balance and found wanting. PERES, your kingdom is divided and given to the Medes and Persians" (5:26–28).

That night Belshazzar was slain and "Darius the Mede received the kingdom" (6:1), making Daniel one of three presidents over the entire empire. The other presidents, jealous of Daniel's successes, induced Darius to forbid petitioning any god or man except him for thirty days, on pain of being cast into a den of lions. Daniel was caught in this trap and the king tried fruitlessly to rescue him, to no avail. With Daniel thrown into the lions' den, the king fasted "and sleep fled from him" (6:19). The next morning the anxious king found Daniel well, to his delight. "So Daniel was taken up out of the den, and no manner of hurt was found upon him because he had *trusted in his God*" (6:24). Daniel's enemies, however, perished in the lions' den. The king then proclaimed that "in all the dominion of my kingdom men tremble and fear before the God of Daniel" (6:27). "So this Daniel prospered in the reign of Darius, and in the reign of Cyrus the Persian" (6:29).

9.2 The Text's Enigmatic Second Half

From Ch. 7 on, the Book of Daniel turns to an account of visions that Daniel had beginning in the first year of Belshazzar's reign. Chs. 7–8 have a distinctively Babylonian character, resembling parts of Ezekiel and the Christian Book of Revelations—full of strange beasts with many horns and the like. Ch. 9 recounts Daniel's supplications in the first year of Darius to the God of Israel, confessing the sins of Israel and pleading for a return to the Land, the Temple, Jerusalem. This material has a typically Judaic character. It was, of course, Cyrus under whom Daniel served that mandated the return. Daniel receives an enigmatic timetable for the return from the angel Gabriel. The rest of the book contains mysterious prophecies involving Persia and Greece and several kings, quasi-historical in character but with an apocalyptic tone. The remarkable end of the text in Ch. 12 cannot be understood until we've made some sense of the rest.

9.3 A Defining Issue: The True Source of Change

At the heart of this bewildering book is a confrontation between the religion of Babylon and the religion of Israel, especially with respect to the issue of change. Its epigram might well be the words of Daniel from Ch. 2: "*He changes the times and the seasons; He removes kings and sets up kings.*" Embodying the Babylonian religion are the sorcerers, enchanters, magicians and astrologers that the kings of Babylonia consulted when confronted with difficulties. Juxtaposed to them are Daniel and his three friends, representing the God of Israel. To understand this encounter requires knowing something of Babylonia's religion. Babylon is famed for being the source of astrology and, to some degree, magic. The worldview behind astrology, still very much with us today, is that the universe is a gigantic machine with the stars and other divinatory sources as the gauges that inform us regarding the cosmic machine's state of affairs. *All change has its source in the cosmic machine.* By consulting the stars, one can foretell the future and find out other pertinent details about changes occurring in the world. For Babylon, the gods themselves were subject to astral fate. Therefore the corps of Babylonian "wise men" and magicians were comparable to experts with a presumed exacting technical *knowledge* of a machine, very much like a refrigerator repairman or an auto mechanic. When a machine isn't functioning properly, the sensible remedy is to call the expert repairman. For Babylonians, especially those of stature, when life isn't functioning properly, one similarly consults those with technical expertise in understanding and adjusting the cosmic machine.

For those like the Babylonians who see dreams as divinatory of the future, bad dreams portend possible negative changes. A mysterious hand writing on the wall is also a frightening portent. Thus Nebuchadnezzar and his son Belshazzar both immediately called in their experts to interpret their troubling experiences. The experts having failed to extract hidden knowledge, both kings then resorted to the renowned Jewish dream and vision interpreter Daniel, who in both instances confirmed that the monarchs' ill omens, in fact, portended very disruptive changes: the loss of their kingdoms—in Nebuchadnezzar's case, only temporarily.

9.4 Knowledge vs. Faith as Remedy for Crisis

For the religion of Daniel and his friends, in contrast with Babylonians, the cosmic machinery was *not* ultimate and knowledge of it even if available was of limited use. The true source of change for them was not the cosmos but its Source—it is the *Creator of the universe who really "changes the times and the seasons."* The Creator was also the only authentic source of information about occurrences in this world. The information, however, could not be accessed at will by some sort of expert human knowledge but rather only received as a gift from Creation's Source. If knowledge is often an appropriate way to fix problems within the Creation—a malfunctioning automobile for example—it is unavailing with respect to relationship with the Creator, Who is beyond the knowledge of His creatures. The fundamental way of relating to the Creator and seeking His help at times of inimical change is through *trust and faith*, as Daniel told Darius after spending a night in the lions' den. Both Daniel and earlier his friends in the fiery furnace were saved not through *knowledge* of the Creation or any aspect of it but by *faith* in the power of the Creator to change even the apparent laws of nature should it suit His purposes. If faith in God can produce miraculous salvation from ordinarily destructive natural forces, how much more so can faith assure the aid of irresistible Divine power when one faces less devastating challenges?

The ultimate power of the Creator is most dramatically illustrated in this text by His removing and setting up kings—ordinarily regarded as wielding supreme earthly authority and might. Yet God reduces Nebuchadnezzar to a grazing bovine and slays his son the same night a warning message is written on the wall. Daniel presents Nebuchadnezzar with a sequence of changes in dominion that would follow his reign, leaving no doubt Who "removes kings and sets up kings." Eventually God is acknowledged as truly the highest Power by Nebuchadnezzar; Darius the Zoroastrian probably had little difficulty believing in a good Supreme Power. Belshazzar, on the other hand, pays the ultimate price for not learning from his father's experience.

9.5 The Status of Esoteric Knowledge within Judaism

But what of knowledge *within* the Judaism of the Book of Daniel? After all, God is touted as a revealer of secrets and the Source of Daniel's interpretive talents. Lest there be any doubt that Daniel's special knowledge is a limited gift from the Creator received by faith, the extraordinarily ironic conclusion of the text wipes all hesitation away. After five or six chapters of largely enigmatic prophetic "foreknowledge," the final word, repeated twice, comes as a slap in the face to those who seek salvation through hidden knowledge or, in Greek, *gnosis*: "But thou, O Daniel, shut up the words and seal the book, even to the time of the end. . . " (12:4); and again, more forcefully: "And I heard, but I understood not; then said I: 'O my lord, what shall be the latter end of these things?' And he said: 'Go thy way, Daniel; for the words are shut up and sealed till the time of the end. . . '" (12:8–9).

The joke, it would appear, is on the radio preachers. All the mysterious apocalyptic utterances of the second half of Daniel are, after all, not available human knowledge, but "till the time of the end" *utterly beyond human grasp* in the spirit of Deuteronomy 30 declaring that "the secret things" belong to the Lord. Here is absolute confirmation, were it needed, that humans are enjoined to look in *faith* to the Creator and not to *knowledge* of the Creation or even of Divine mysteries for all their needs, for it is indeed He Who "changes the times and the seasons" and, through His Divine Providence, "removes kings and sets up kings." What could underscore this more emphatically and surprisingly than the candidly declared inaccessibility of presumed prophetic "knowledge" that has occupied almost half the text! This sealed book seems almost to mock those who would endeavor to reach hybristically beyond their human station.

9.6 Daniel's Place within the Ketuvim

No better succinct description of the Book of Daniel's scriptural function could be devised than the one prefigured for it: *the theoretical basis for dealing with disruptive change in life.* Disruptive change afflicts the lives of virtually all the major players in this saga—kings, wise men, Jews and their enemies alike. The theoretical principle for dealing with it, beyond any doubt, is stalwart faith in the God of Daniel, the Creator of heaven and earth, even in the face of what seems certain destruction. Our job is to *exercise our faith* and maintain our corollary conviction in the salvific ways of *Divine Providence*—saving us is God's business, even if the threat on occasion is a fiery furnace or a den of lions. It is now evident why Divine Providence plays so prominent a role in Ruth and Esther, although God Himself remains hidden: alertness to such Providence is the chief practical application of Daniel's presentation of its theoretical centrality.

There is no change within the Creation that is beyond the power of the Creator to effect, however miraculous the Divine action might appear to mortal eyes. And there is no change within the Creation that does not have its true source with the Creator. Armed with conviction of the transcendent, absolute and providential power of God over both nature and history, persons may be well prepared to meet the disruptive crises that overtake them as they go about the practical business of living—as do Ruth and Esther. When even the staunchest faith seems unavailing, admittedly it may be time to turn from Daniel back to Job that faith might be reinforced. But with these three intimately related final texts unlocked, the door is open for those so moved to incorporate all the Ketuvim we have studied into their daily experience: together these texts appear to offer nothing less than Divine counsel for the largest questions—the "boundary questions"—that our free, innermost spirits face as earthly beings made in the image of God: together, nothing less than a universal spiritual handbook of Abrahamic monotheism.

The Question of Revelation: An Epilogue

FAITH in Abrahamic scripture as revealed truth is generally considered a private religious matter, not directly related to the interpreted meaning of texts. But our study of the Ketuvim, excluding only the four generically historical books because of their functional distinction, may inject this issue with new and more public urgency that challenges the limits of the interpreter's task:

Alternative Possibilities: Human Construct, Chance, Providence

The obvious, yet astonishing, fact is that the nine texts we have examined were canonized as scriptures due to acceptance of their individual spiritual merit over a number of centuries. Within the tradition, they have always been presumed to be a miscellaneous collection with a variety of authors, having little in common apart from acknowledged special sanctity, diversity and failure to conform to the other two genres of Hebrew scriptural literature. Their only acknowledged generic similarity is that they are accorded a lesser degree of inspiration than the other two sections of Tanakh. Consider the supportive comment of Brevard Childs, a renowned Christian scholar well versed in Rabbinic sources and considered an acknowledged master on the subject of canonization:

"Modern critical scholarship has attributed little significance to the Hebrew canon's division of a final section called the Writings or Hagiographa. The reasons for this evaluation are not difficult to discover. . . the third division of the Hebrew canon appears to be a catch-all which lacks coherence. Even those subsections which do exhibit some degree of inner relationship, such as the five *Megillot* [read on particular Judaic holy days], derive this unity from a post-Talmudic liturgical practice, and contribute little to the interpretation of the Hebrew text (Childs, 501–502)." Certainly the Ketuvim are not placed in any evident categorical order in the Tanakh, unlike—for example—the clear division established between major and minor prophets or the historical ordering of the five books of Torah. Neither does the Torah tradition, from the Talmud onward, endeavor to ascribe any system or architectonic structure to them, even though it extensively discusses their canonization. As Childs notes, modern scholarship certainly does not tease out such a structure; it is in full accord with Torah tradition's own judgment.

Accordingly, the pattern upon which this analysis has stumbled was *entirely unlikely* to have been devised as a conscious and deliberate act by a human editor or any group of redactors. The unlikelihood is confirmed when one considers that there is no inkling in the entire Judaic tradition, including Kabbalah, that such a pattern exists. This position of Judaic tradition is echoed plainly by Christian and secular scholarship, as exemplified by Brevard Childs above. To appreciate this fully, it is vital to note that the pattern is *not at all esoteric* in any way but at the "plain surface" of the text—*p'shat* in Talmudic terms. If the tradition had grasped the pattern, there would have been no imaginable reason not to have made it as explicit as the patterning of Torah and Nevi'im since it illumines the basic meaning of the texts: it is evident that the ordering of Torah, the Pentateuch, is straightforwardly chronological, and the ordering of the Nevi'im, the Prophets, is generic with the three major and twelve minor prophets grouped together. Surely there would have been no reason not to present the Ketuvim in a similar orderly fashion as likewise an aid to comprehension—*if that order had been understood.*

The unlikelihood of the pattern being humanly devised is

further increased when one considers that the schema reflects a peculiarly contemporary mode of philosophical and structural thinking unlikely to have been accessible to antiquity. Indeed, the hypothesis of stability and change as probable poles of the horizontal axis was suggested by a common ground of the systems of ancient Greek, Indian, and Chinese thought: this highly abstract, high-level insight is accessible only through the comparative philosophy of religion, a subdiscipline still in its infancy whose roots are no more than a century or so old. Without the aid of the comparative philosophy of religion, it would have been virtually impossible to have hit upon an appropriate polarity to characterize the relation among the five Ketuvim texts dealing with relation to the Creation.

Supported by the above considerations, in addition to one's own informed perception as an interpreter, we suspect that most readers would agree that once the organizing schema elaborated upon herein has been discerned, it nonetheless appears so imbued with intentionality and indeed inevitability that it becomes *untenable to construe the relationship between the nine texts in any other way*. These nine texts *do*, in fact, constitute a perfectly crafted guide to understanding and dealing with the four most basic two-fold existential challenges shaping human life: closeness with the Creator, distance from the Creator, stability in the Creation, change in the Creation. The texts are as sharply defined in relation to one another as the facets of a diamond. In addressing the reader, they speak also to one another with profound resonance that deepens with continued study.

Thus there is no escaping the question of how this elegant organizing schema can be explained. The probability of *chance* accounting for the nine literary-philosophical texts' (out of the Ketuvim's thirteen) displaying such an orderly structural interrelation is statistically infinitesimal. We likened it to a bucket of sand thrown in the air, coming down to form an exquisite landscape on the sidewalk. Therefore, unless one is persuaded by some characterization of a merely human if mysterious collective unconsciousness working in obscurity over an expanse of centuries, there seems little alternative to the claim of tradition itself: *that these are texts of revealed truth, providentially selected and only now (as tradition could not foresee) made fully understandable.* Discovery of an embedded but entirely inobvious pattern testifies to the inspired character of textual content as well as organizing structure.

For only a transcendent Mind, endowed with the mysterious power to orchestrate history providentially, could have discerned the four basic and universal spiritual challenges to humanity and inspired texts that address them with a precision as undeniable as it is uncanny—all the while unbeknownst to their authors and compilers working over several centuries. As to the question of "why now," Torah tradition affirms that there are aspects of Torah that can be grasped only when the time is right. And, indeed, a unifying handbook of fundamental and universal Abrahamic monotheism could hardly be more necessary than at the present historical moment, when the three main Abrahamic traditions may be poised on the verge of mutual annihilation. Here, then, is arguably also evidence for a living Lord Who is not so much *philosophical*, i.e., Hellenic, as deeply *historical*, i.e., Hebraic.

As always with faith, the issue cannot be forced. Those who have the eyes see. Those who do not can always find a way to excuse themselves. Nonetheless, what many will concur in recognizing as a plainly visible instance of timely discovery—some might agree in saying providential revelation—can only feel strengthened and emboldened in the summons to deeper fellowship among those who acknowledge and worship the One God of Abraham—a God of Providence Who brings each thing "in its season" and Who seeks nothing more fervently than the unity of eschatological peace among His human children: a God Who apparently wishes that peace delayed no longer.

Contemplating the Ketuvim

For those convinced of the evidence of revelation in the structure explicated herein, the Ketuvim present the possibility of an auxiliary method to complement whatever other spiritual practices a person may currently be engaged in. This may be particularly important for the Abrahamic trialogue, which invites Jews, Christians and Muslims to actively seek deeper forms of fellowship. A spirituality of the Ketuvim might be divided into the Contemplation of Form and the Contemplation of Content.

Form: This entire book documents the discovery of an aspect of Divine revelation unrecognized until now and, arguably, not fully *necessary* to grasp until now when the three Abrahamic traditions are in unprecedented need of communing with one another by virtue of being able to affirm a common Divine Source. To ponder the process by which this structural aspect of revelation became disclosed, and to consider the precision with which each text of the Ketuvim performs its assigned task in a hitherto unsuspected way, can become a contemplation of the reality of revelation and its Revealer. This can lead to an ever deepening recognition of the workings of Divine Providence in governing the world as it has guided the shaping of revelation. To begin with, the timely and providential disclosure of the pattern would seem to be a seal of authentification testifying to the revealed character not only of the Ketuvim but of the entire Tanakh. It offers a springboard to considering that the prophetic words in Nevi'im and the supreme revelation of the Torah itself are truly of supernatural Divine origin. It may suggest ways to Jews and Christians to consider the possibility of inspiration in the Qur'an. As an Abrahamic believer ponders how Providence has operated to infuse spiritual awareness ever more deeply into consciousness, one can anticipate an epiphanic moment of recognition—of awakening—at which the believer becomes able more confidently to understand and embrace the reality of an omniscient, omnipotent Providential God as a unassailably solid fact of reality.

Content: The Contemplation of Form concludes with the deep, internalized, indubitable conviction that the Ketuvim are truly revealed texts and that the supernatural Abrahamic God of revelation is entirely real. In the Contemplation of Content, the believer slowly and carefully studies each text, relating it to its paired text, to the texts at the opposite poles, ultimately to the entire array of nine books. Such a study could be ongoing over a number of years and could be conducted individually and/or in pairs/groups. The goal here is to appropriate, absorb and ingrain the teachings more and deeply until they become part of one's very being. Eventually one's actions will be spontaneously informed by the wisdom of the Ketuvim without one's having to take conscious thought. Then any Abrahamic believer will be living more intensely and genuinely than ever before in the presence of the living God. And the Fellowship of Abraham will have put down deep roots in the hearts of all the faithful.

Appendix One: Building the Fellowship of Abraham

If the astonishingly precise organizing schema of these nine texts of the Ketuvim implies a Divine source of their revelation, then the disclosure of the schema in these post-World War II decades of turmoil must likewise bear the imprint of Divine Providence. This Providence underscores that the outreach towards one another of some of the children of Abraham, even as others feud more bitterly than ever before, may indeed be in response to a momentous historical summons of the God of Abraham. It seems that those who would follow the God of Abraham are being called to exert themselves in every way possible to establish a fellowship that just could be a vital seed of the long awaited rule of God on earth. Surely it takes no zealotry for believers to recognize in the unprecedented crises of our age likely birthpangs (*chevlei ha-Mashiach*) of the Final Redemption (*Ge'ulah Sh'leimah*)—to use the Hebrew terminology.

But what might be concretely entailed in building the Fellowship of Abraham? The first step has already been taken: steps toward trialogue, an initial gathering of Jews, Christians and Muslims in many areas of the world, endeavoring to see one another as indeed children of Abraham and seekers after his One God. This book may itself constitute a second step, unveiling a *foundational text* through which Abrahamic monotheists may begin to deepen their affinity and sense of community. Heretofore there has been no sacred text that Jews, Christians and Muslims could conscientiously study together. And that already implies what remains to be done: the next necessary move is expansion of the impulse toward Fellowship through communication among different widely dispersed groups and the attracting of more and more participants. Here the computer, to some the ensign of humanism's often arrogant secular ideal of self-sufficiency, may prove an instrument of providential intent.

The Fellowship of Abraham requires a universally open home in the only public place possible—cyberspace: it needs a *website.* It takes little exertion of imagination to envision how such a website might function. Most importantly, it would offer a mechanism for locating nearby Fellowship groups and for such groups to interact with one another. This could operate, for example, through the input of a county and state. Software might then identify Fellowship groups—large and small, formal and informal, affiliated with houses of worship and unaffiliated—throughout not only the indicated county but adjacent counties or even states. Contact information would be provided. In this way, interested individuals could find Fellowship groups and the groups themselves might connect with one another to develop larger regional groupings on the way toward national and international visibility and effect.

Interaction among groups would facilitate further concrete steps of joint spiritual growth. These may include the study of other texts, the development of joint liturgies and prayers, the devising of social action toward implementing the humane ethics of Abraham and His God. A website or several could support all of this by offering bibliographies, chatrooms, personal connections around common interests, and so forth. The Prayer constituting the next appendix, for example, would surely be a website posting. Modern technology has removed all limits to the degree of cooperation and significant mutual acquaintance open to likeminded people.

Ultimately such human efforts can fructify only if sanctioned and blessed by the God of Abraham. But the signs of the times suggest that these efforts might indeed fulfill His present intent. And an ever more global Fellowship of Abraham must hope and pray that at some point its actions will provide God with some of the critical human contributions necessary to a Divine design for bringing history to the unifying consummation of universal peace and fellowship that God has surely intended from the beginning.

Appendix Two: A Prayer to the God of Abraham

Elokei Avraham, God of Abraham, Illah Ibrahim—God of the one by whom, according to Scripture, shall "all the families of the earth be blessed"—

In the Tanakh, sacred to Jews, we read: "Did I not bring up... the Syrians from Kir?" We also read: "In that day Israel will be the third with Egypt and Assyria, a blessing in the midst of the earth, whom the Lord of hosts has blessed, saying, 'Blessed be Egypt my people, and Assyria the work of my hands, and Israel my heritage.'" These passages teach that each people, even those formerly at odds, has its unique place and precious value within the design of creation—a harmonious place that will in the endtimes, by God's providential workings, become fully manifest and known to all.

In the Gospel, sacred to Christians, we read that God's house has "many mansions." We also read "Blessed be the peacemakers..." and "Love thine enemies." These passages suggest that the ways in which God works with each people may not be known to or grasped by others, yet we should value and love one another despite misunderstandings.

And in the *Qur'an*, sacred to Muslims, we read "Dispute ye not, unless in kindliest sort, with the people of the Book...and say ye, 'We believe in what hath been sent down to us and hath been sent down to you. Our God and your God is One...'" We also read "...on the resurrection day, God shall judge between [the peoples of the Book] as to that in which they have differed." These passages instruct that, until the mystery of our differences is illumined at the endtimes, all peoples who acknowledge and seek the God of Abraham should especially honor and embrace one another as spiritual kin.

And yet, O God, Who called Abraham to the path of blessing, Whose essence is merciful love and Whose Face is to the East and to the West alike, we confess our abject failure to find the Way of peace together. For many centuries, those who profess to seek You have pridefully disdained one another and continuously caused others pain, thus dishonoring Your Name, violating Your intent, defying Your redemptive design.

We therefore, still wishing to be true followers of Abraham, turn to You, O God, to humbly beseech Your help in grasping the deeper truths of the paths we believe You have shown us. We implore You to draw our minds, hearts and hands into complete surrender to You. We ask that you open our spirits to the one convergent path of peace, mutual respect and joint striving in the way of active goodness toward the day when unto You alone shall every knee bow, when You will be All in All, when every person—whether turning to the East or the West—will recognize only Your Face.

Liberate our souls from fear so that they may be filled with love, especially with affectionate regard for all who seek genuinely to worship You. Purify our spiritual communities and help us to shape them into a vast Fellowship of Abraham that will begin to learn, even in the midst of the differences which You have presently ordained, how to serve the One God as one great family of Abrahamic peoples. Open the hearts of those who resist so that they may acknowledge and embrace the way of active goodness toward the time when "nation shall not lift up sword against nation, neither shall they make war anymore." Above all, hasten the day when without compulsion your Name shall be One throughout the world You have created. Bring us now, O God we pray, in eager recognition and submission to Your true path of shalom, peace, salaam.

May the One Who creates peace in the heights above establish peace among us, throughout the entire Fellowship of Abraham and in the midst of all humankind.

Amin, amen, amein

About the author

Charles Vernoff (1942–2013) was professor of religion at Cornell College from 1978 until his retirement in 2006, where he was integral in reshaping the curriculum of his department. He was an undergraduate at the University of Chicago, and a graduate student at Harvard University, the University of California at Santa Barbara, and the University of Jerusalem, and completed his Ph.D. at UC Santa Barbara.

His childhood experiences with Judaism, Christianity, and Hinduism set him on the path "of a destined comparative religionist" from an early age, to use his own words. Throughout his career at Cornell, Vernoff published numerous articles in *Journal of the American Academy of Religion*, *Journal of Ecumenical Studies*, *Jewish Civilization: Essays and Studies*, and more. His two books, *For the Children of Abraham: Scripture's Widsom* and *Shabbat*, were published posthumously by Ellipsis Imprints.

Also available from
Ellipsis Imprints
• • •

❧ *Shabbat* by Charles Vernoff

In Vernoff's own words, "the mission of this book to illumine the character of Shabbat, the heart of Judaism, as gateway to transcendence." In seeking this illumination of a central component of Judaism, Vernoff wrestles with the very question of what it means to be a Jew.

❧ *Striking Bodies, Striking Minds* edited by Sara L. Uckelman

Stories, poetry, songs, art, and more from the 2018, 2019, and 2020 higher education strikes in the United Kingdom. Proceeds from the sale of this charity anthology are donated to the Universities and Colleges Union Fighting Fund.

For more information, go to
`http://www.ellipsis.cx/~liana/ellipsisimprints/`
or visit us on Twitter: `@EllipsisImprint`

CPSIA information can be obtained
at www.ICGtesting.com
Printed in the USA
LVHW050800130422
716028LV00014B/709

9 781838 072339